EASY PIANO

50 Songs for Children

ISBN 0-634-02525-2

HAL•LEONARD®
CORPORATION
7777 W. BLUEMOUND RD. P.O. BOX 13819 MILWAUKEE, WI 53213

Visit Hal Leonard Online at
www.halleonard.com

A-TISKET A-TASKET

Traditional

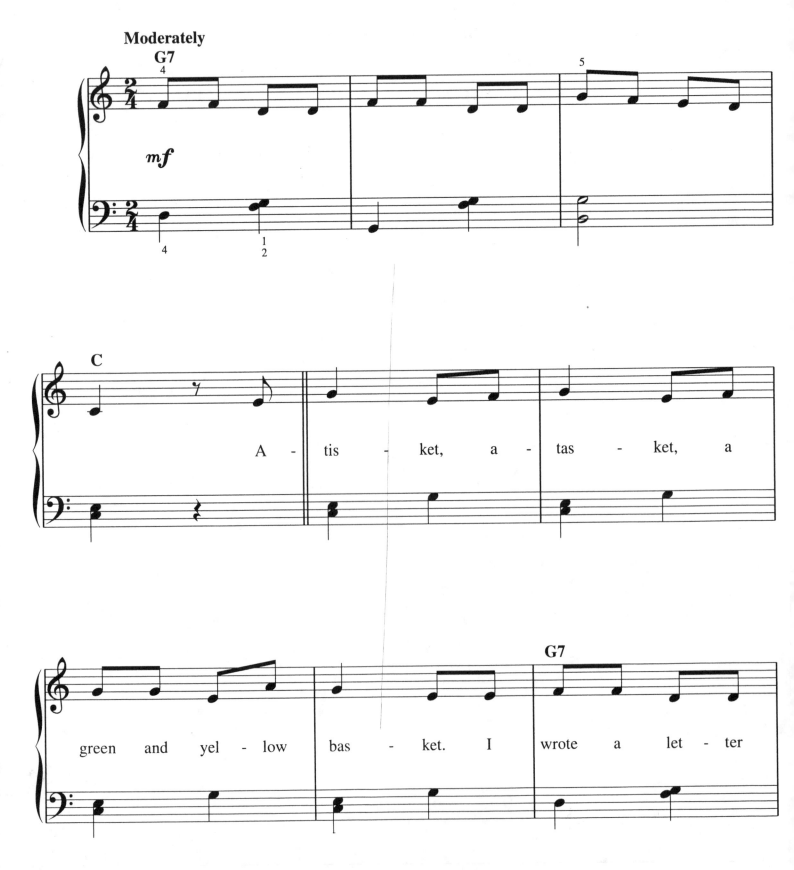

to my love and on the way I dropped it. I

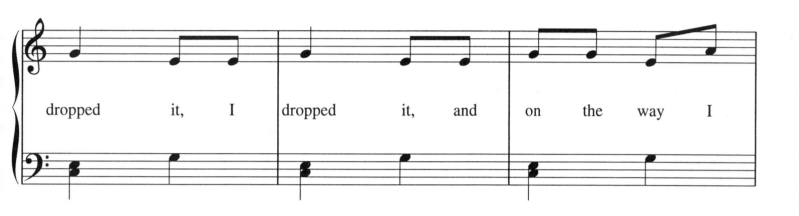

dropped it, I dropped it, and on the way I

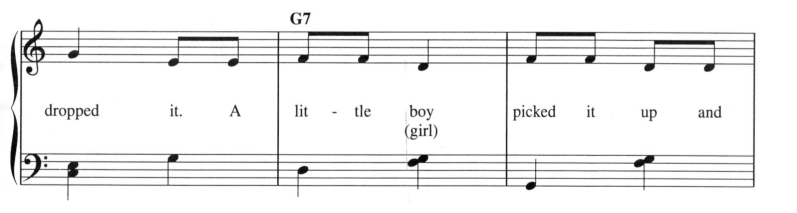

dropped it. A lit – tle boy picked it up and
(girl)

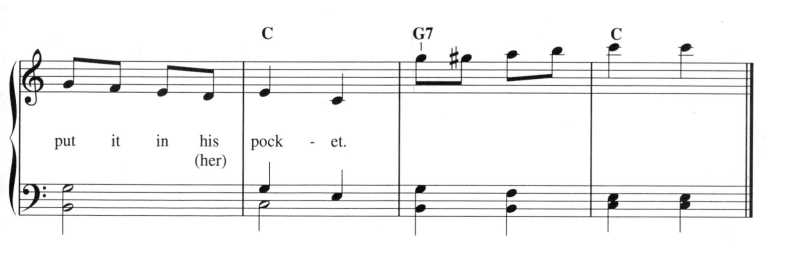

put it in his pock – et.
(her)

ANIMAL FAIR

American Folksong

Moderately

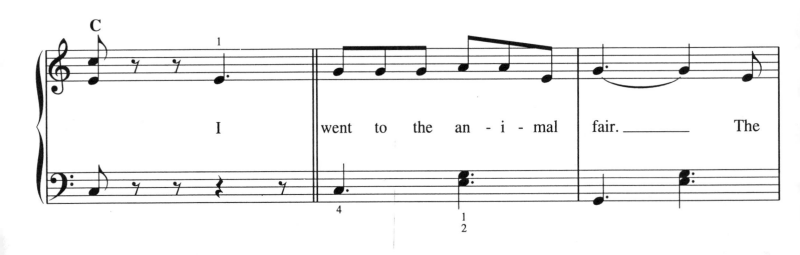

I went to the an - i - mal fair. _____ The

birds and beasts were there. _____ The big ba - boon, by the

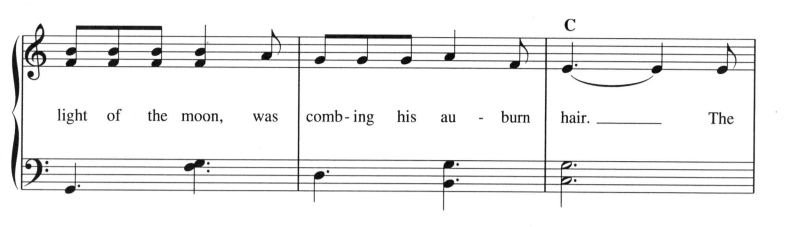

light of the moon, was comb-ing his au - burn hair. _____ The

mon - key, he got drunk, _____ and sat on the el - e -phant's

trunk. _____ The el - e - phant sneezed, and fell to his knees, and

what be - came of the monk, the monk, the monk, the monk?

ALPHABET SONG

Traditional

BAA BAA BLACK SHEEP

Traditional

BE KIND TO YOUR WEB-FOOTED FRIENDS

Traditional

Bright March Tempo

THE BEAR WENT OVER
THE MOUNTAIN

Traditional

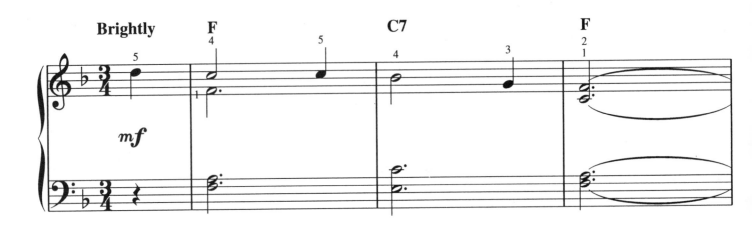

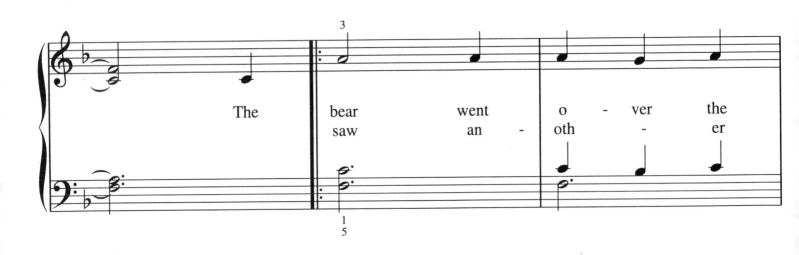

The
bear went o - ver the
saw an - oth - er

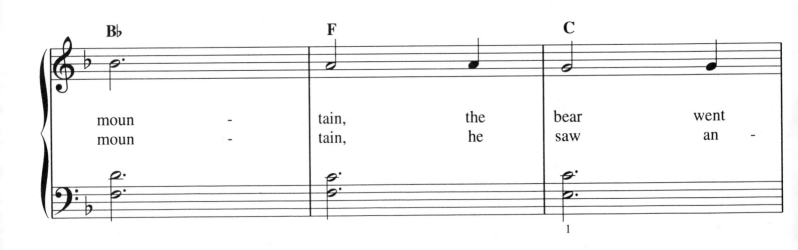

moun - tain, the bear went
moun - tain, he saw an -

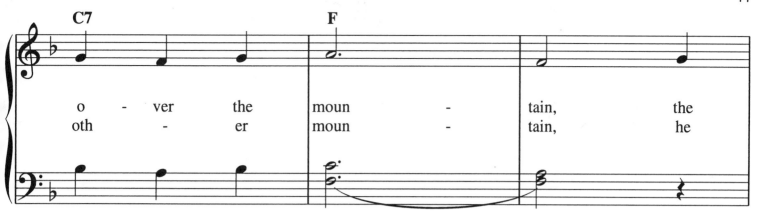

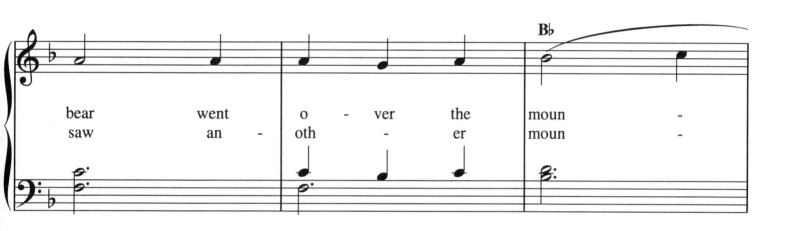

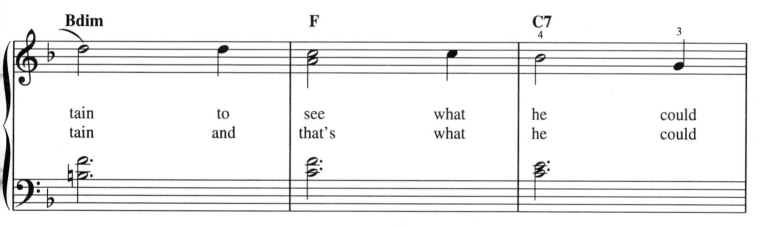

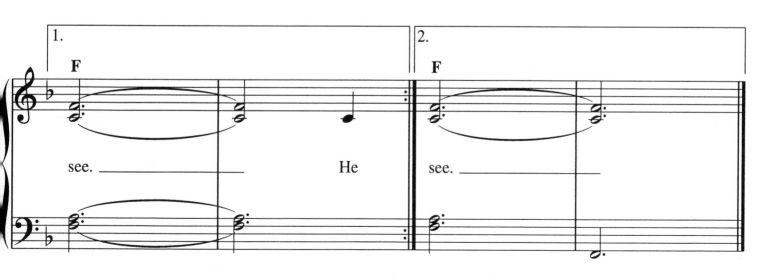

BINGO

Traditional

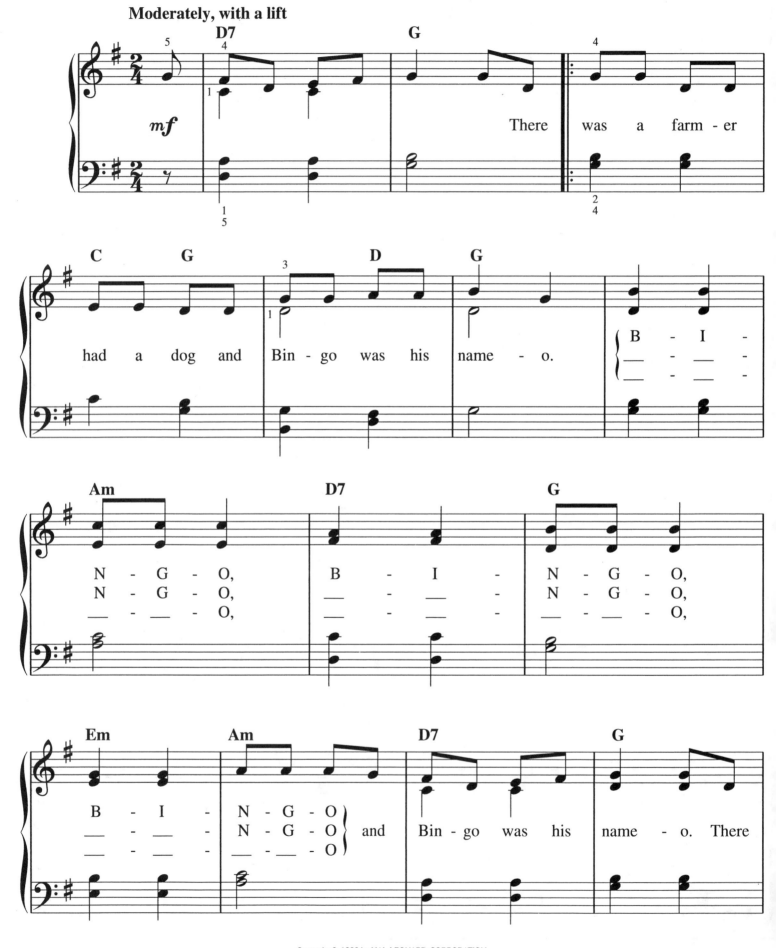

DO YOUR EARS HANG LOW?

Traditional

DRY BONES

Traditional

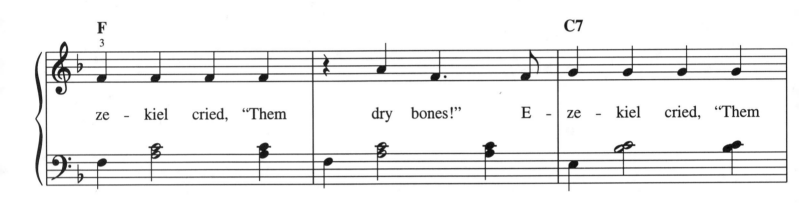

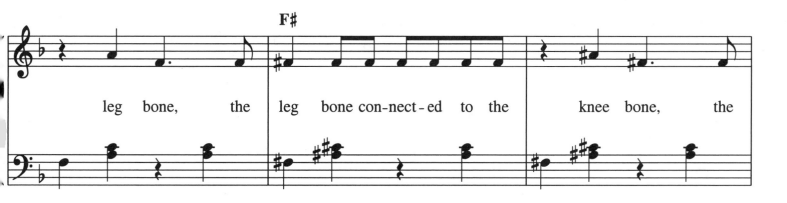

leg bone, the leg bone con-nect-ed to the knee bone, the

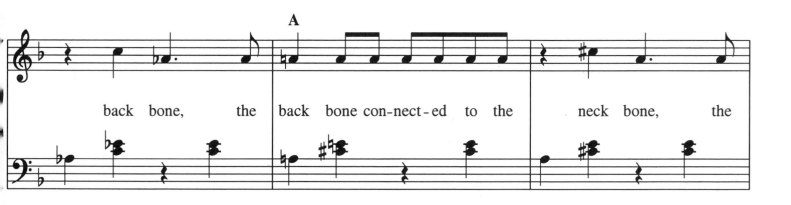

knee bone con-nect-ed to the thigh bone, the thigh bone con-nect-ed to the

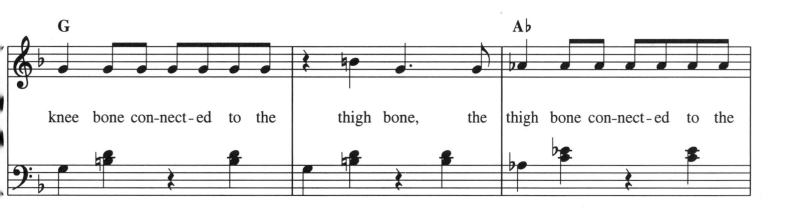

back bone, the back bone con-nect-ed to the neck bone, the

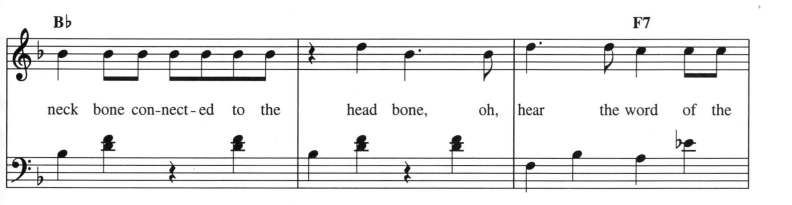

neck bone con-nect-ed to the head bone, oh, hear the word of the

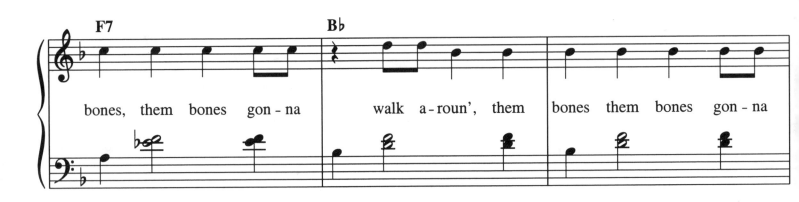

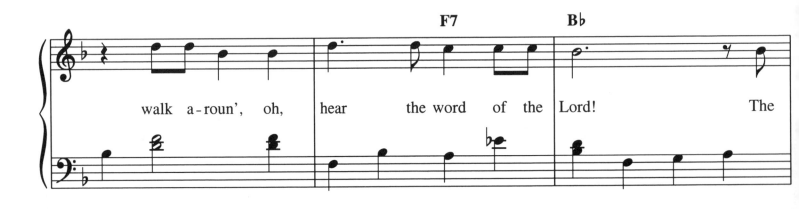

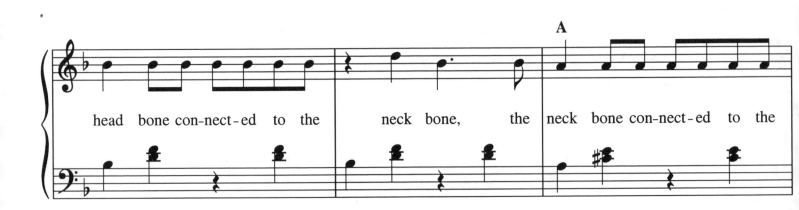

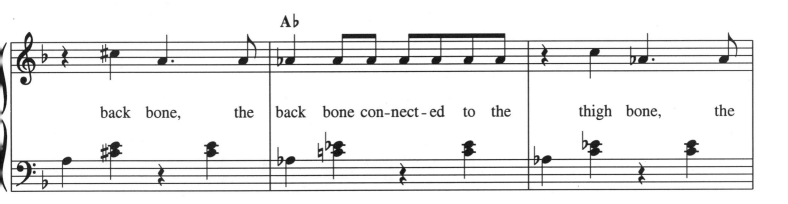

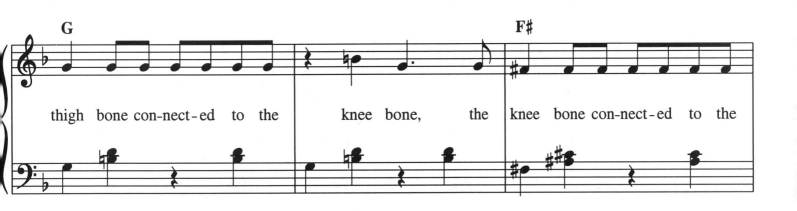

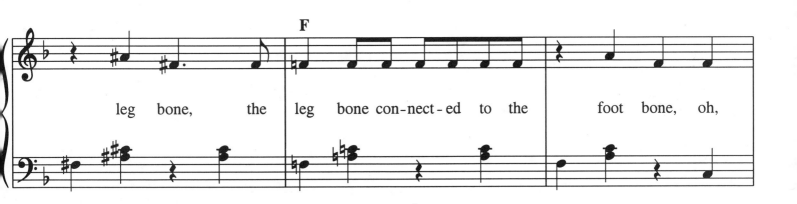

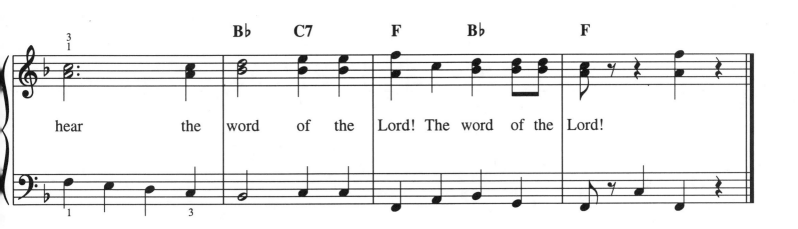

DOWN IN MY HEART

Traditional

joy,   joy,   joy,   joy,   down in   my

C   **C♯dim**   **D7**

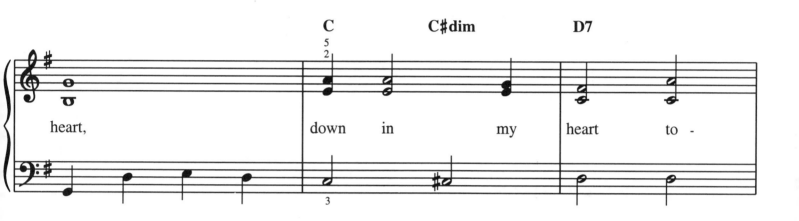

heart,   down in   my   heart   to -

G   **G7**   **C**

day.   I've got that   peace that pass - eth

un - der - stand - ing   down in   my   heart,

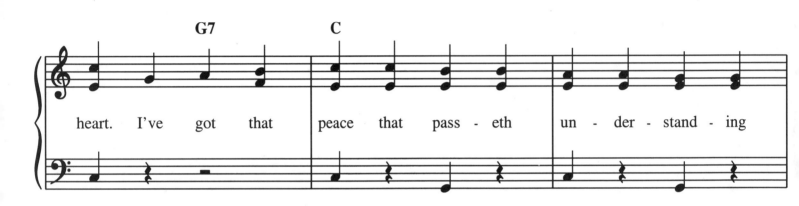

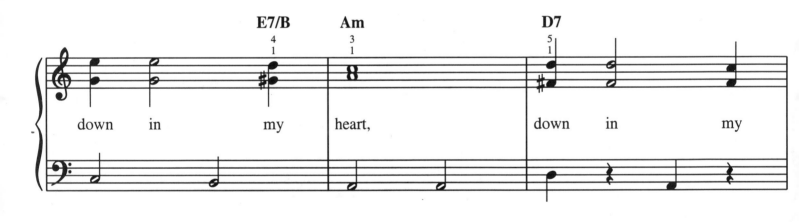

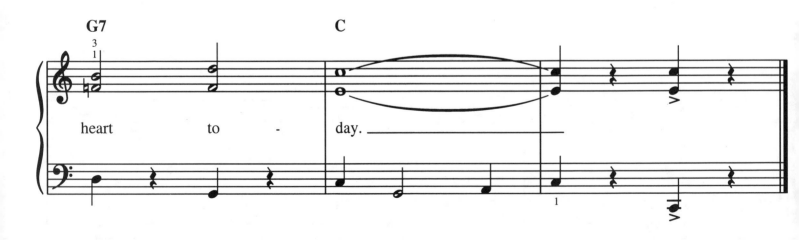

EENSY WEENSY SPIDER

Traditional

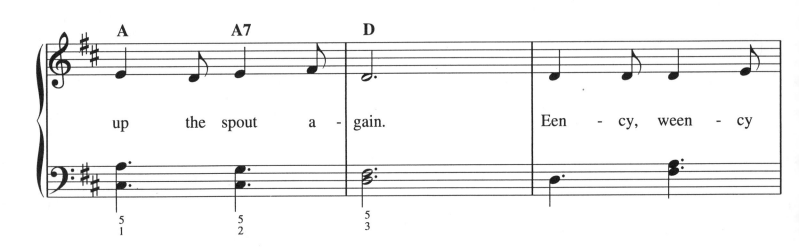

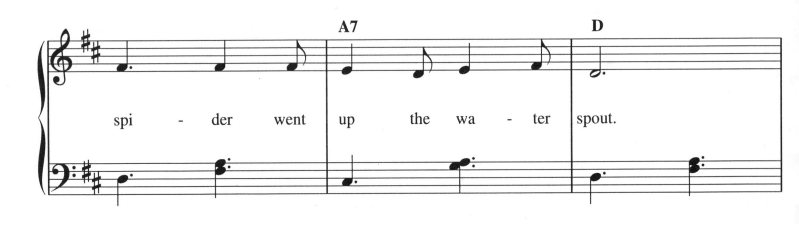

24

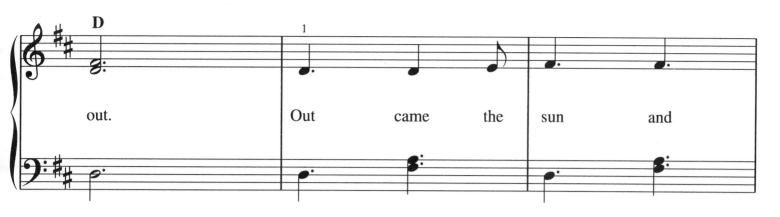

out.   Out   came   the   sun   and

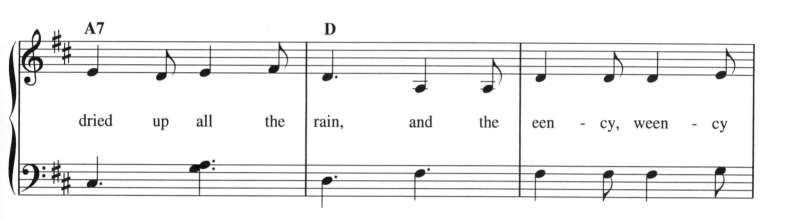

dried   up   all   the   rain,   and   the   een - cy, ween - cy

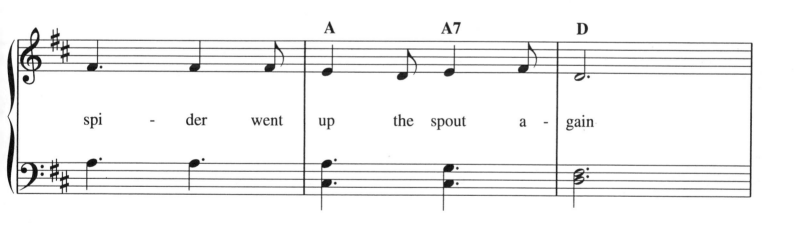

spi - der   went   up   the   spout   a - gain

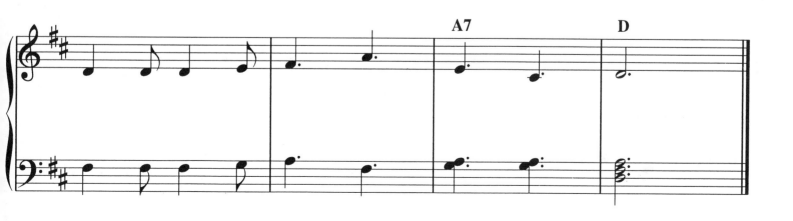

THE FARMER IN THE DELL

Traditional

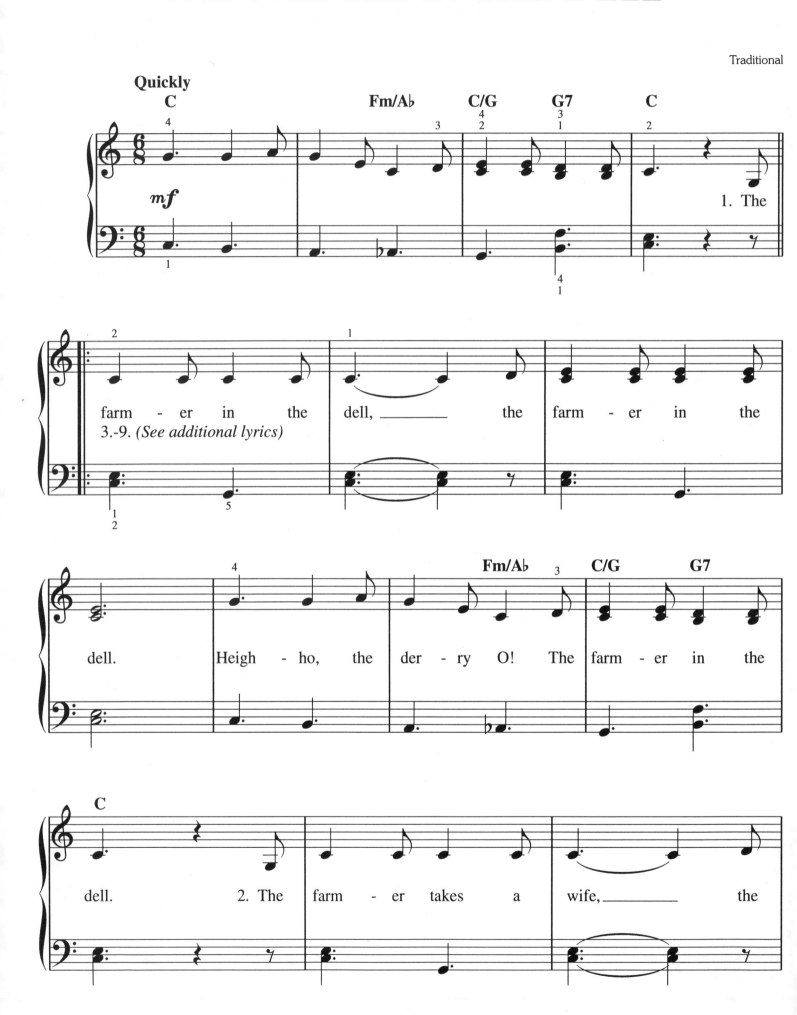

farm - er takes a wife. Heigh - ho, the

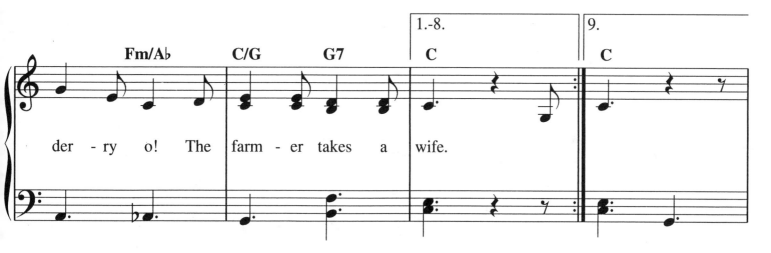

der - ry o! The farm - er takes a wife.

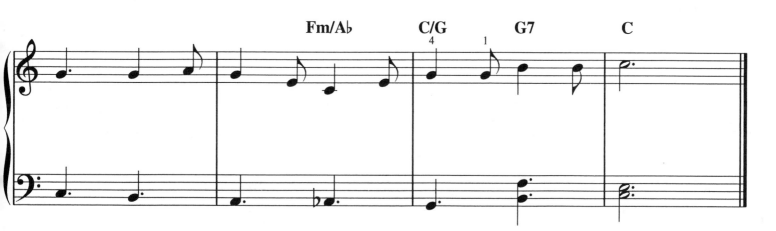

Additional Lyrics

3. The wife takes the child,
   The wife takes the child,
   Heigh-ho, the derry o!
   The wife takes the child.

4. The child takes the nurse,
   The child takes the nurse,
   Heigh-ho, the derry o!
   The child takes the nurse.

5. The nurse takes the dog,
   The nurse takes the dog,
   Heigh-ho, the derry o!
   The nurse takes the dog.

6. The dog takes the cat,
   The dog takes the cat,
   Heigh-ho, the derry o!
   The dog takes the cat.

7. The cat takes the rat,
   The cat takes the rat,
   Heigh-ho, the derry o!
   The cat takes the rat.

8. The rat takes the cheese,
   The rat takes the cheese,
   Heigh-ho, the derry o!
   The rat takes the cheese.

9. The cheese stands alone,
   The cheese stands alone,
   Heigh-ho, the derry o!
   The cheese stands alone.

FOR HE'S A JOLLY GOOD FELLOW

Traditional

For he's a jol-ly good fel-low, for
won't go home un-til morn - ing, we

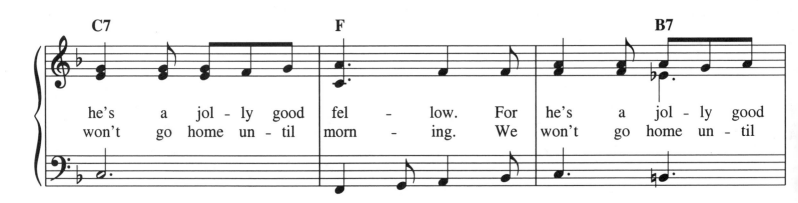

he's a jol-ly good fel - low. For he's a jol-ly good
won't go home un-til morn - ing. We won't go home un-til

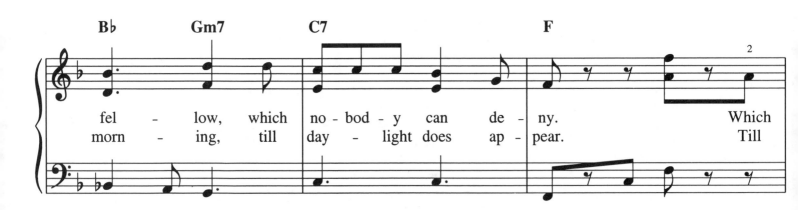

fel - low, which no-bod-y can de - ny. Which
morn - ing, till day - light does ap - pear. Till

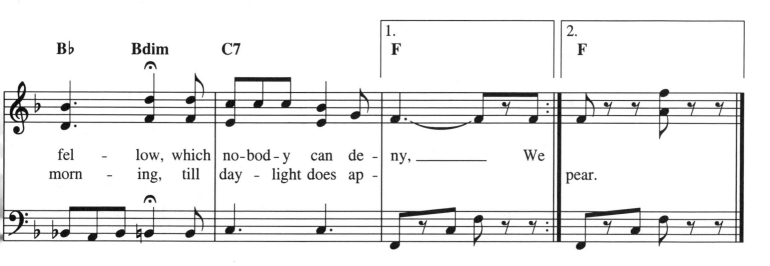

FRÈRE JACQUES
(Are You Sleeping?)

Traditional

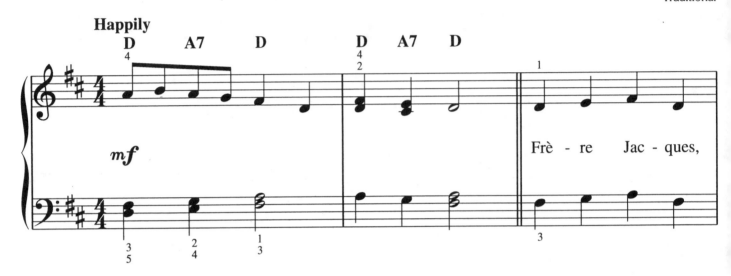

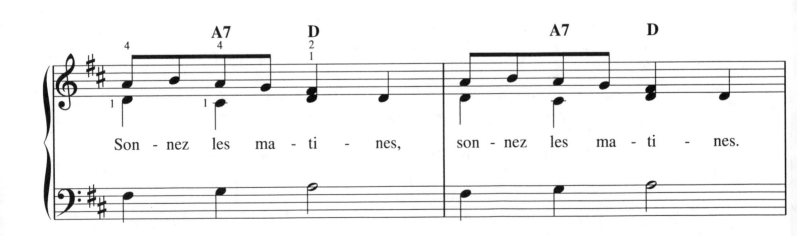

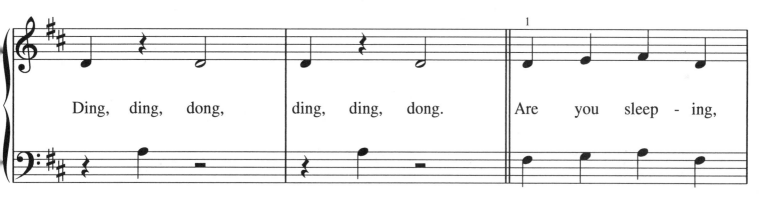

Ding, ding, dong,   ding, ding, dong.   Are you sleep - ing,

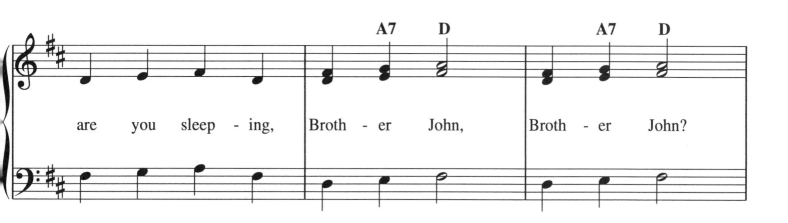

are you sleep - ing,   Broth - er John,   Broth - er John?

Morn-ing bells are ring - ing,   morn-ing bells are ring - ing.   Ding, ding, dong,

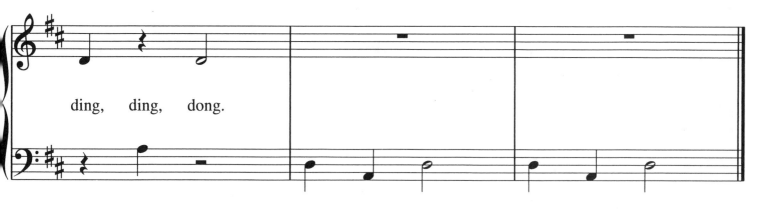

ding, ding, dong.

GRANDFATHER'S CLOCK

By HENRY CLAY WORK

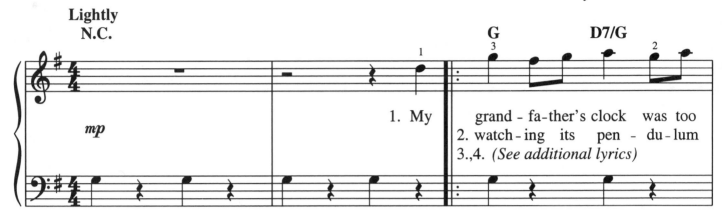

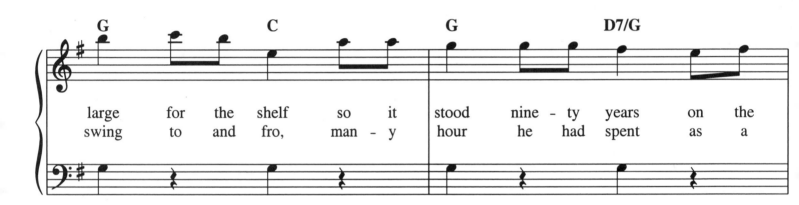

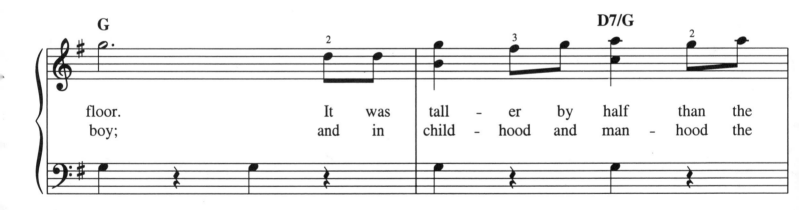

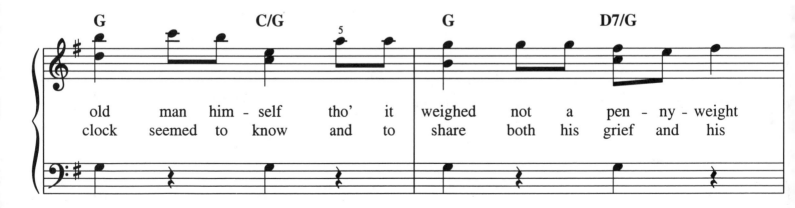

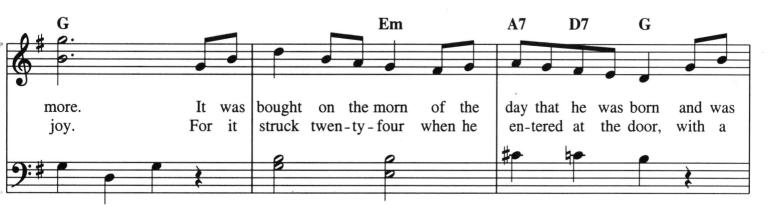

more.   It was bought on the morn of the   day that he was born   and was
joy.   For it struck twen-ty-four when he   en-tered at the door,   with a

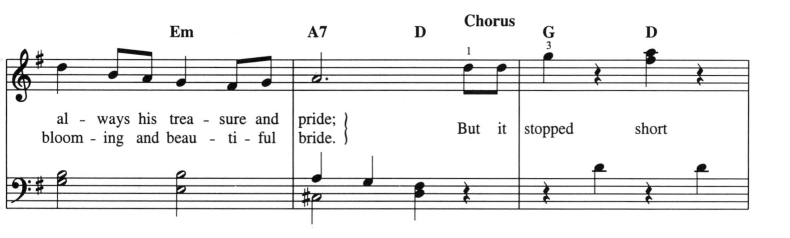

al - ways his trea - sure and   pride; ⎱   But   it stopped   short
bloom - ing and beau - ti - ful bride. ⎰

Chorus

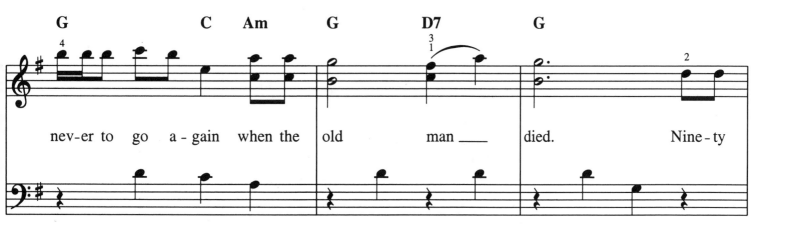

nev-er to go a-gain when the   old   man ___ died.   Nine-ty

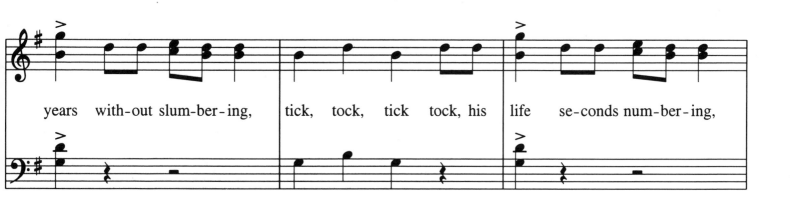

years with-out slum-ber-ing,   tick, tock, tick tock, his   life   se-conds num-ber-ing,

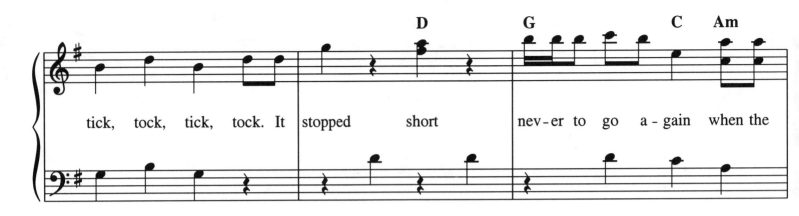

tick, tock, tick, tock. It stopped short nev-er to go a-gain when the

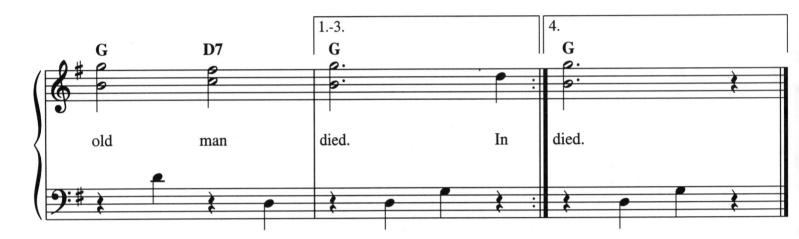

old man died. In died.

Additional Lyrics

3. My grandfather said that of those he could hire,
Not a servant so faithful he found;
For it wasted no time, and had but one desire,
At the close of each week to be wound.
And it kept in its place, not a frown upon its face,
And its hands never hung by its side.
Chorus

4. It rang an alarm in the dead of the night,
An alarm that for years had been dumb;
And we knew that his spirit was pluming its flight,
That his hour of departure had come.
Still the clock kept the time, with a soft
and muffled chime,
As we silently stood by his side.
Chorus

IT'S RAINING, IT'S POURING

Traditional

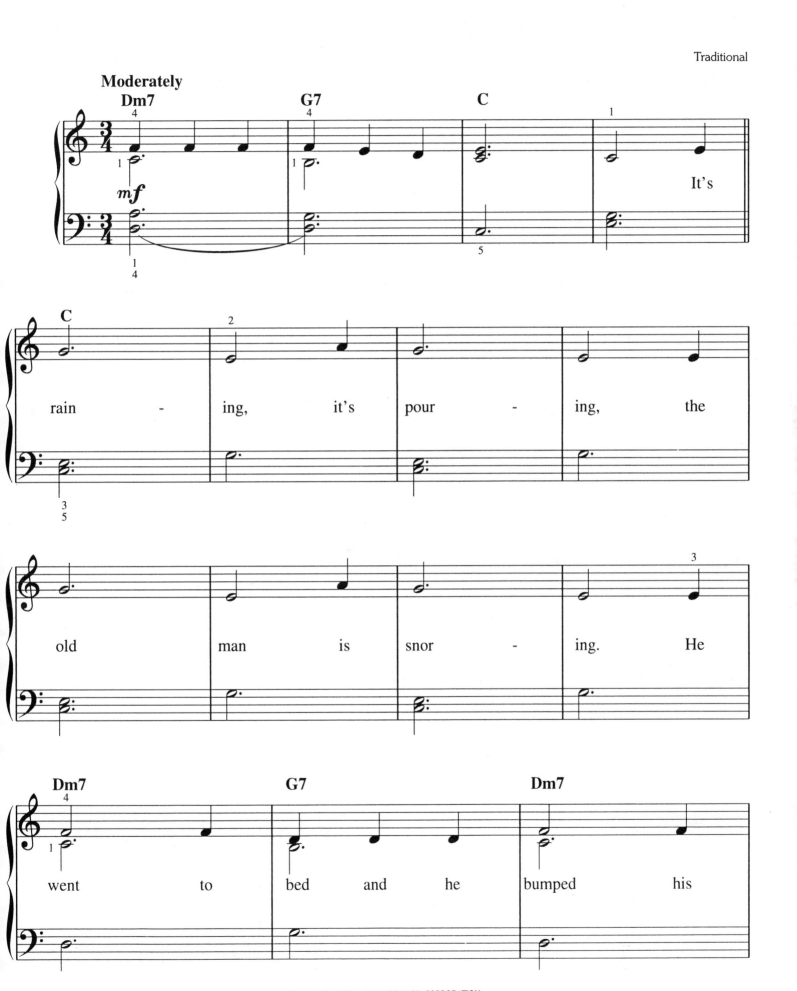

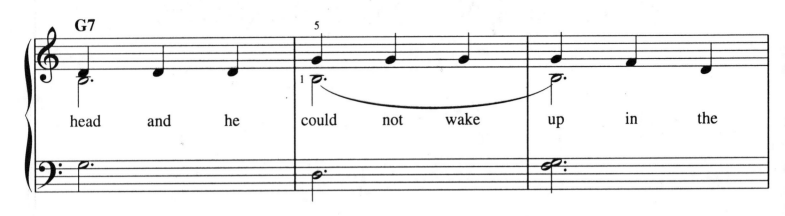

G7

head   and   he   could   not   wake   up   in   the

C

morn   -   ing.   It's   rain   -

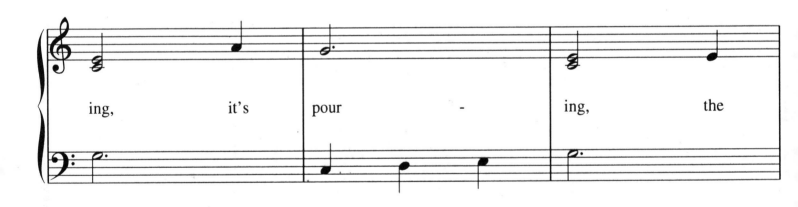

ing,   it's   pour   -   ing,   the

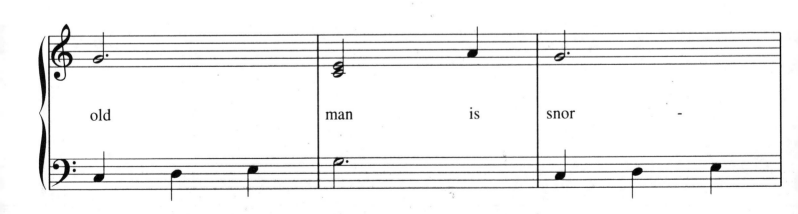

old   man   is   snor   -

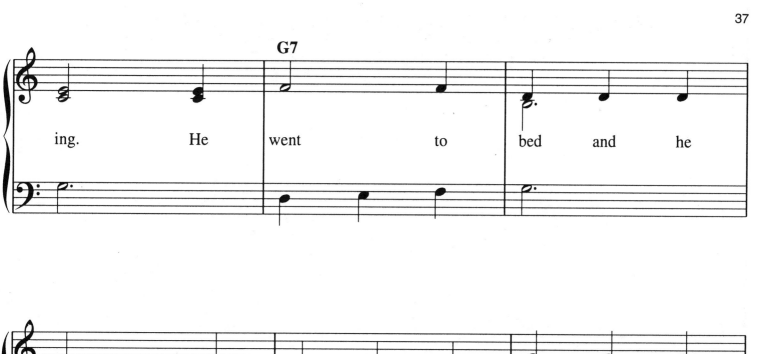

ing.   He   went   to   bed   and   he

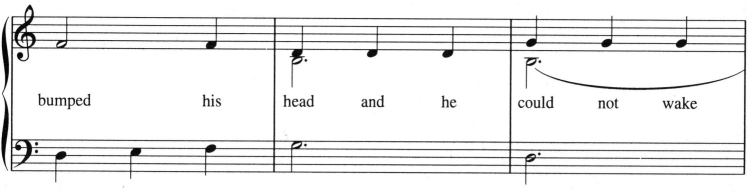

bumped   his   head   and   he   could   not   wake

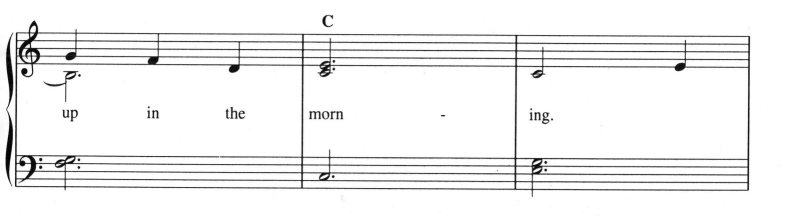

up   in   the   morn -   ing.

HE'S GOT THE WHOLE WORLD IN HIS HANDS

Traditional Spiritual

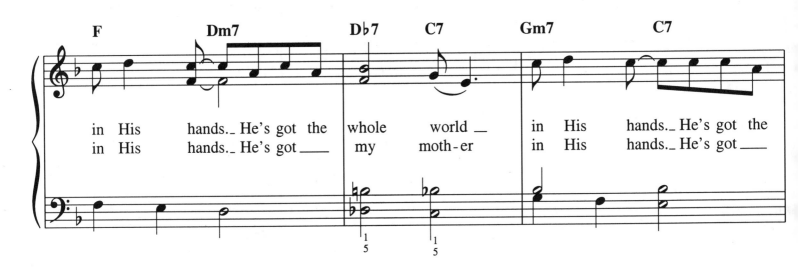

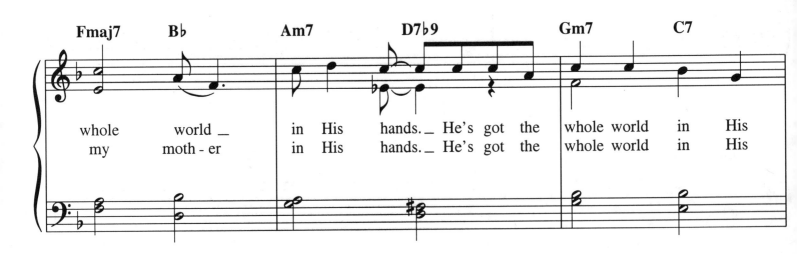

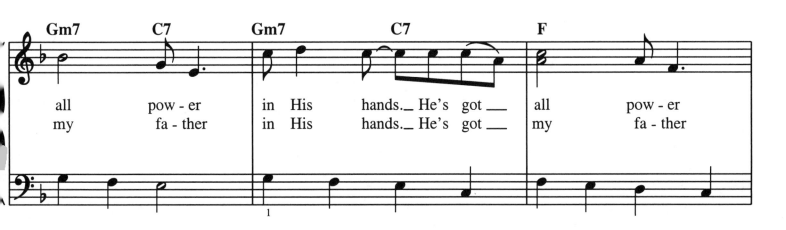

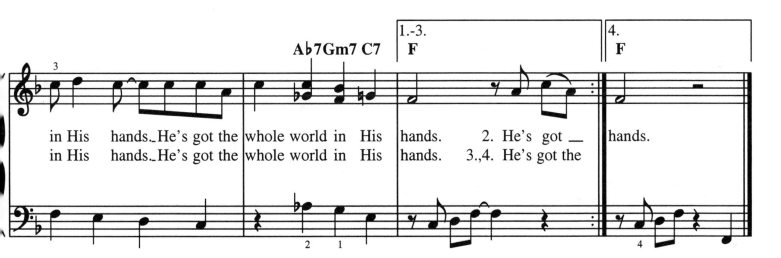

Additional Lyrics

3. He's got the whole church in His hands.
   He's got the whole church in His hands.
   He's got the whole church in His hands.
   He's got the whole world in His hands.

4. He's got the whole world in His hands.
   He's got the whole world in His hands.
   He's got the whole world in His hands.
   He's got the whole world in His hands.

HOME ON THE RANGE

Moderately

Lyrics by DR. BREWSTER HIGLEY
Music by DAN KELLY

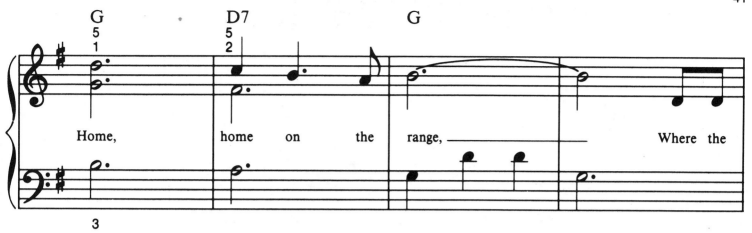

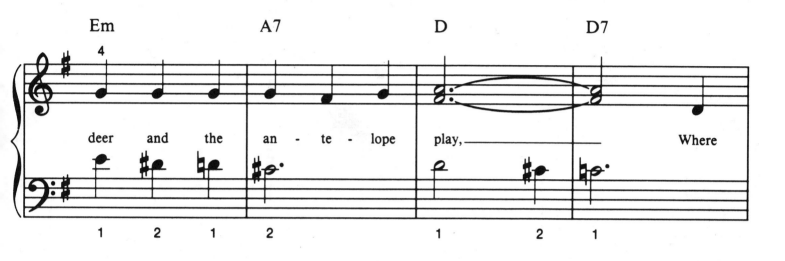

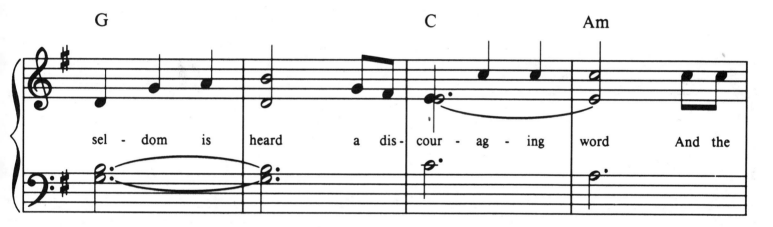

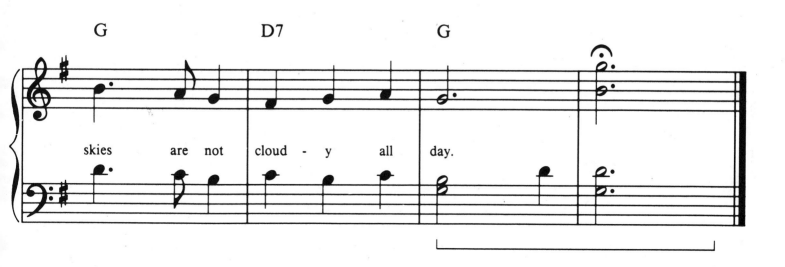

HUMPTY DUMPTY

Traditional

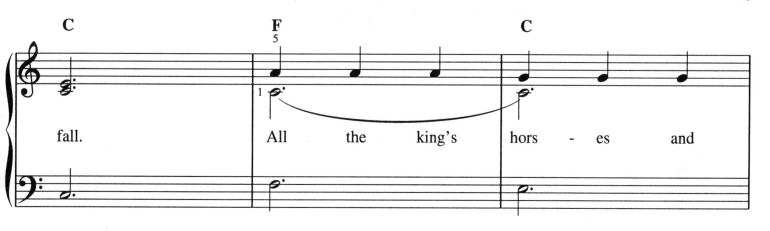

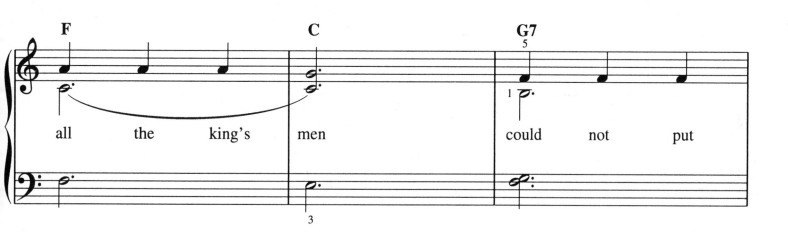

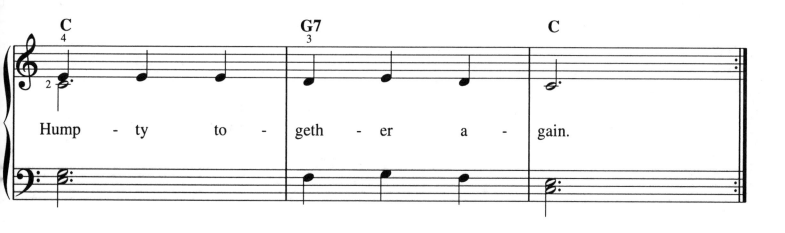

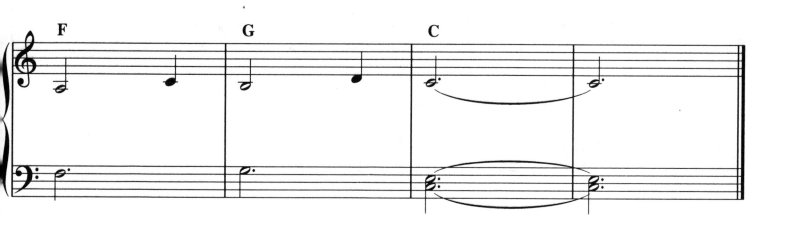

HUSH, LITTLE BABY

Carolina Folk Lullaby

Additional Lyrics

3. If that jumping jack won't hop,
   Papa's gonna buy you a lollipop.
   When that lollipop is done,
   Papa's gonna buy you another one.

4. If that lollipop is all eaten up,
   Papa's gonna buy you a real live pup.
   If that puppy dog won't bark,
   Papa's gonna buy you a meadow lark.

5. Hush, little baby, don't say a word.
   Papa's gonna buy you a mockingbird,
   And if that mockingbird don't sing,
   Papa's gonna buy you a diamond ring.

6. If that diamond ring is glass,
   Papa's gonna buy you a cup of brass,
   And from that cup you'll drink your milk,
   And Papa's gonna dress you in the finest silk.

7. Yes, Papa's gonna dress you in the finest silk,
   And Mama's gonna raise you with honey and milk,
   So hush, little baby, sleep safe and sound;
   You're still the sweetest little babe in town.

I'VE BEEN WORKING ON THE RAILROAD

American Folksong

I've been work-ing on the rail - road, all the live - long day. I've been work-ing on the rail - road, just to pass the time a - way. Can't you hear the whis - tle blow - in'?

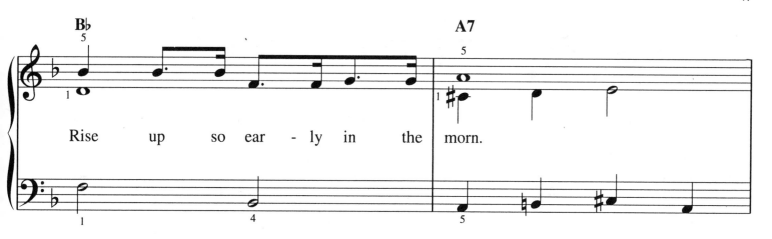

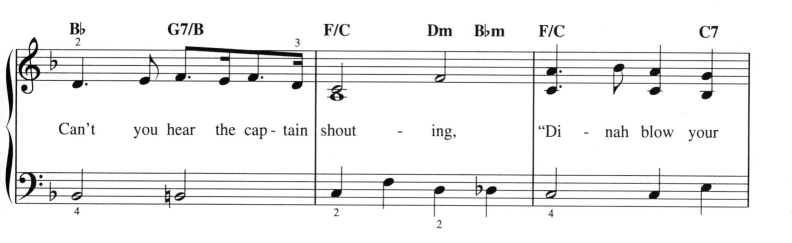

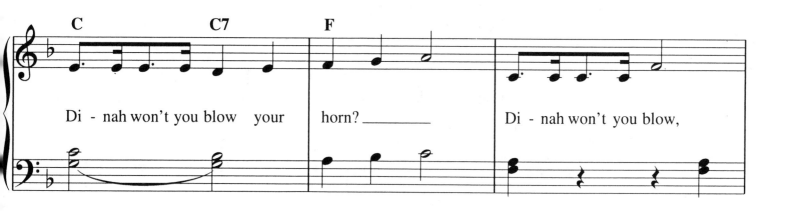

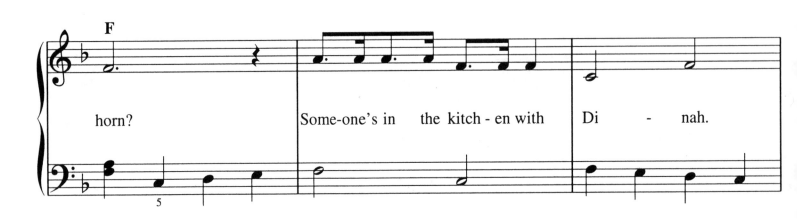

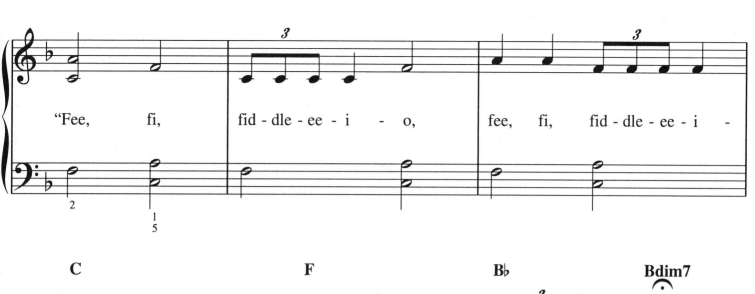

"Fee, fi, fid - dle - ee - i - o, fee, fi, fid - dle - ee - i -

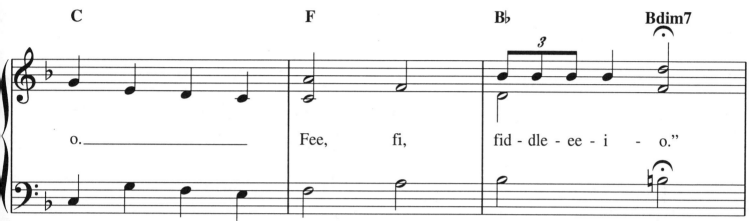

| C | F | B♭ | Bdim7 |

o. _____ Fee, fi, fid - dle - ee - i - o."

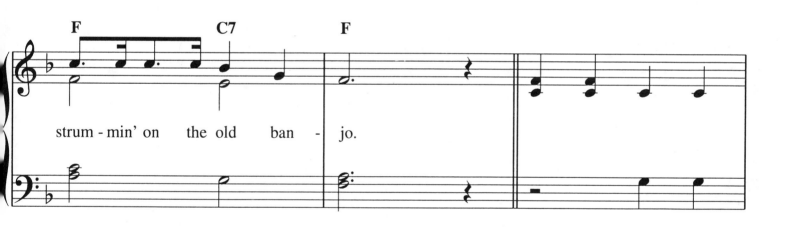

| F | C7 | F | |

strum - min' on the old ban - jo.

| | C | G C7 | F |

IF YOU'RE HAPPY AND YOU KNOW IT

Words and Music by
L. SMITH

JACK AND JILL

Traditional

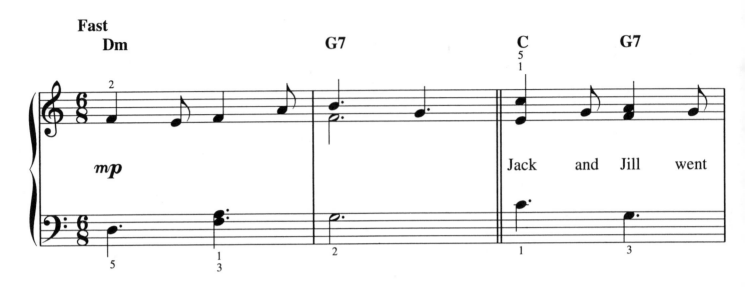

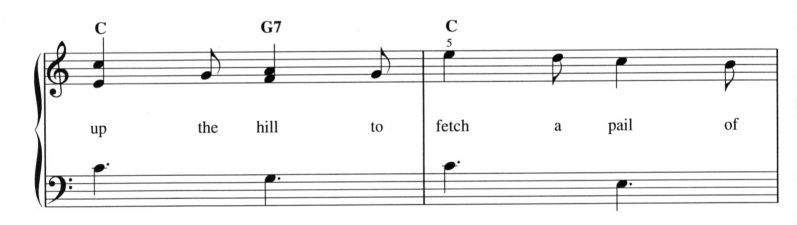

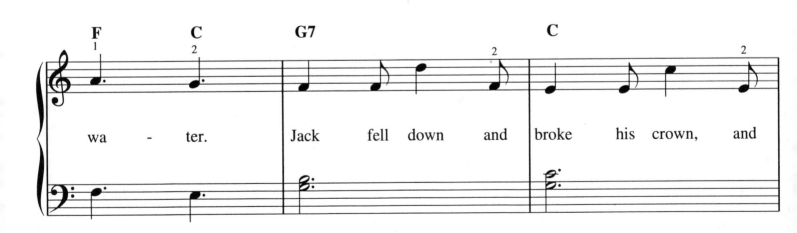

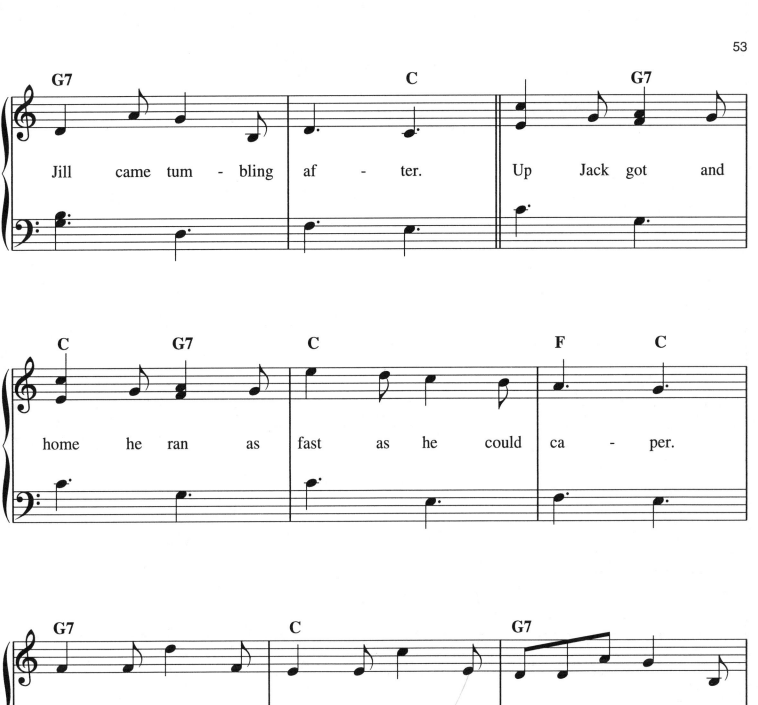

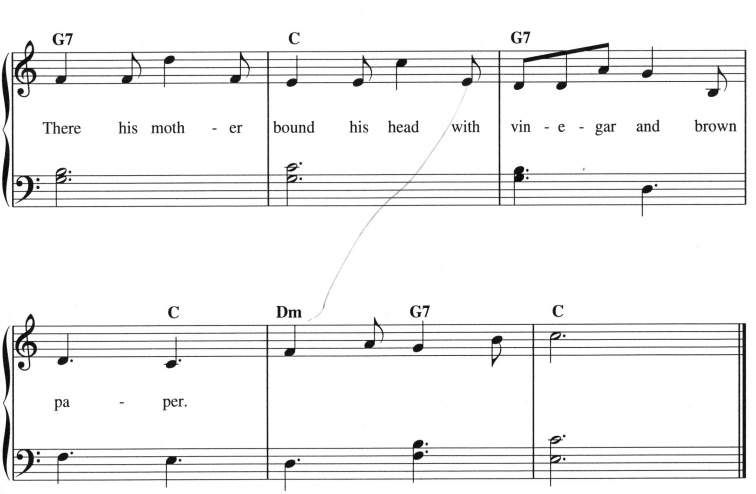

JOHN JACOB JINGLEHEIMER SCHMIDT

Traditional

OH! SUSANNA

Words and Music by
STEPHEN C. FOSTER

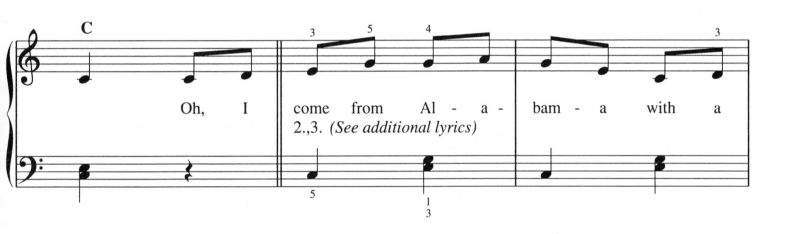

Oh, I come from Al - a - bam - a with a

2.,3. *(See additional lyrics)*

ban - jo on my knee. And I'm goin' to Lou' - si -

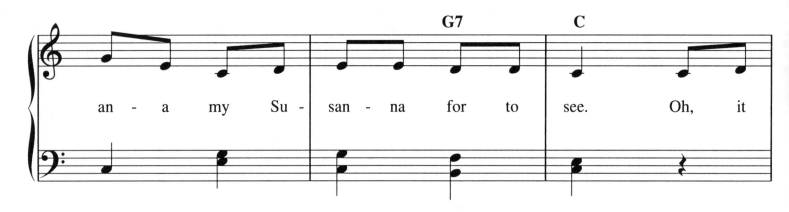

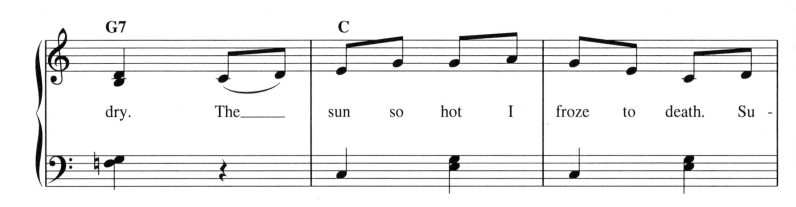

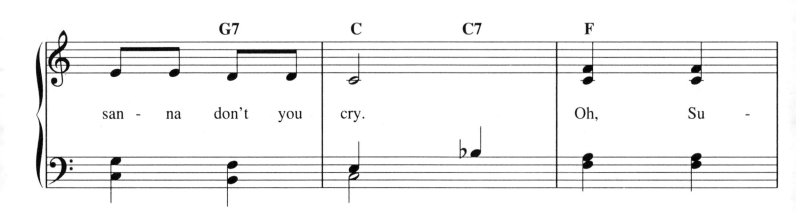

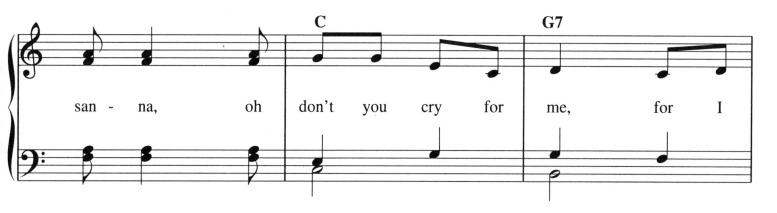

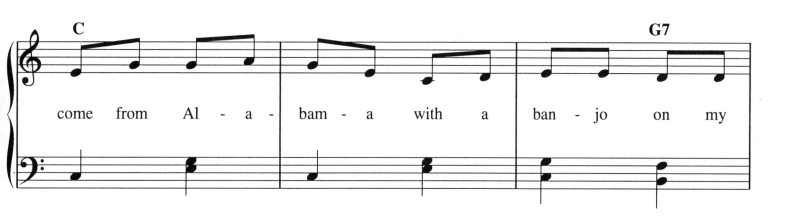

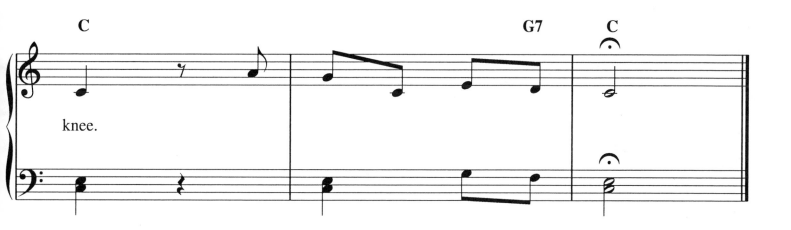

Additional Lyrics

2. I had a dream the other night
When everything was still.
I thought I saw Susanna
A-coming down the hill.

3. The buckwheat cake was in her mouth,
The tear was in her eye,
Say I, "I'm coming from the South,
Susanna, don't you cry."

LONDON BRIDGE

Traditional

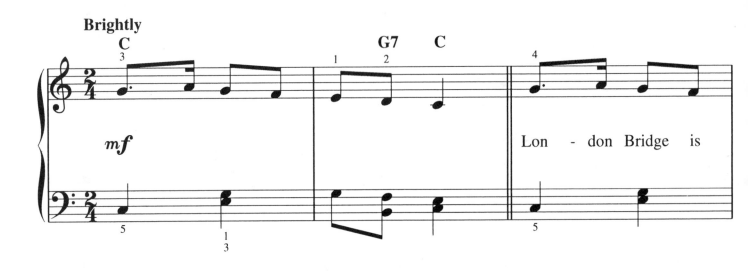

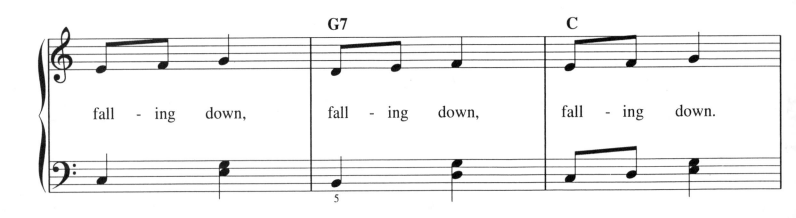

MARY HAD A LITTLE LAMB

Words by SARAH JOSEPHA HALE
Traditional Music

Ma - ry had a lit - tle lamb, lit - tle lamb,
fol - lowed her to school one day, school one day,

lit - tle lamb. Ma - ry had a lit - tle lamb, its
school one day. It fol - lowed her to school one day, which

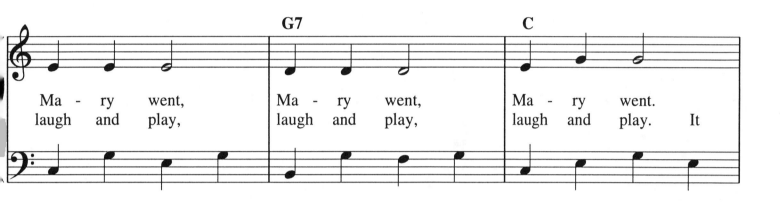

MICHAEL ROW THE BOAT ASHORE

Traditional Folksong

THE MUFFIN MAN

Traditional

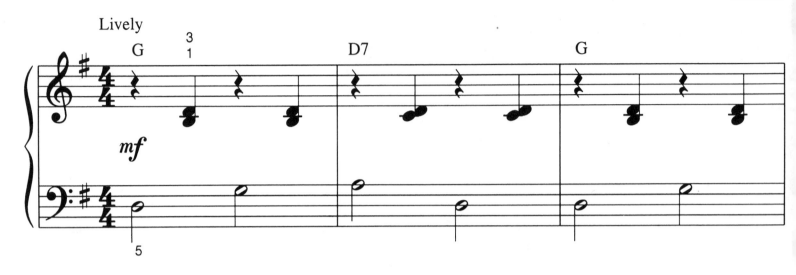

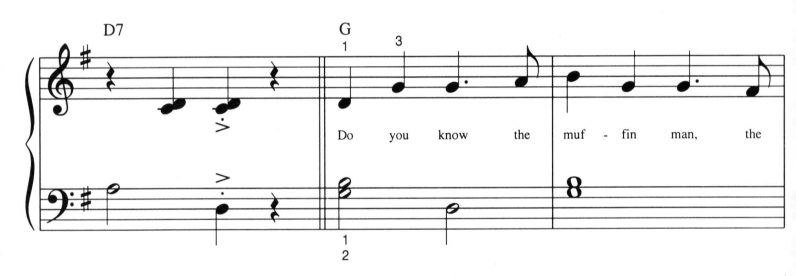

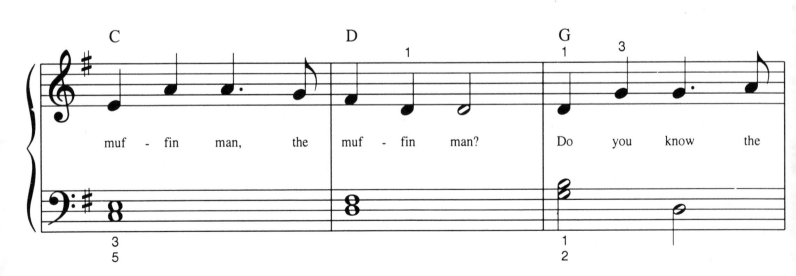

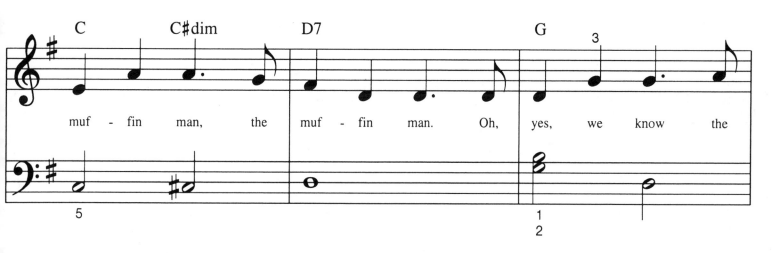

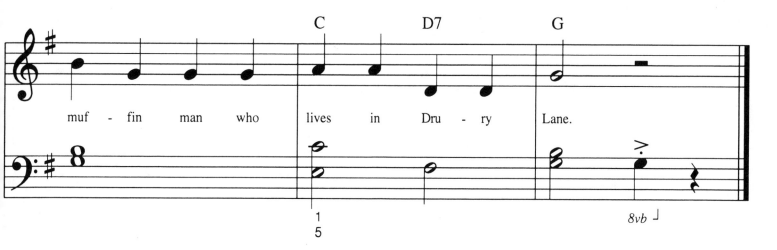

MY COUNTRY, 'TIS OF THEE

(America)

Words by SAMUEL FRANCIS SMITH
Music from *Thesaurus Musicus*

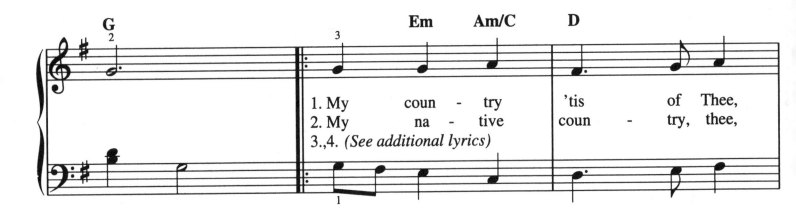

1. My coun - try 'tis of Thee,
2. My na - tive coun - try, thee,
3.,4. *(See additional lyrics)*

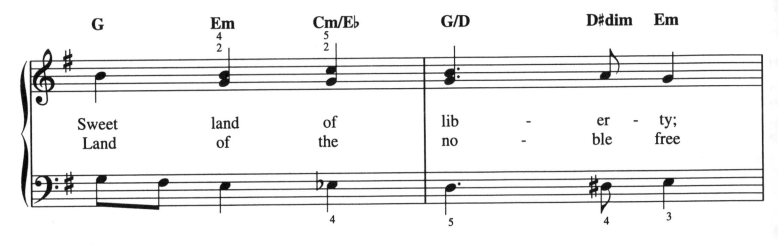

Sweet land of lib - er - ty;
Land of the no - ble free

Of Thee I sing.
Thy name I love;

Land   where   my   fa -   thers died   Land   of   the
I   love   thy   rocks   and   rills   thy   woods   and

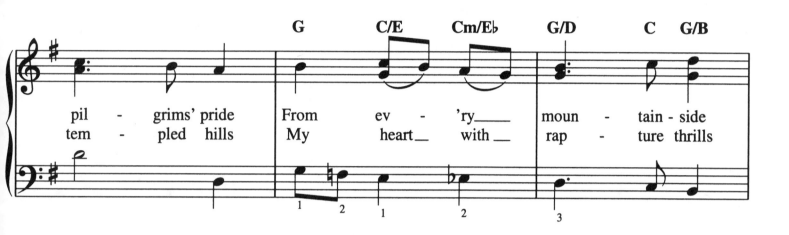

G   **C/E**   **Cm/E♭**   **G/D**   **C**   **G/B**

pil -   grims' pride   From   ev -   'ry____   moun -   tain - side
tem -   pled   hills   My   heart__ with __ rap -   ture thrills

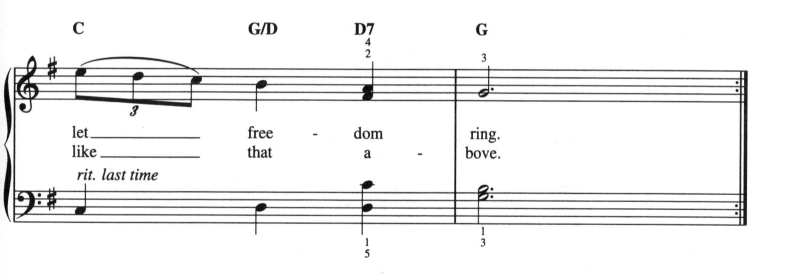

C   **G/D**   **D7**   **G**

let_____   free -   dom   ring.
like _____   that   a -   bove.

rit. last time

Additional Lyrics

3. Let music swell the breeze
   And ring from all the trees
   Sweet freedom's song.
   Let all that breathe partake
   Let mortal tongues awake
   Let rocks their silence break
   The sound prolong.

4. Our fathers' God, to thee
   Author of liberty
   To Thee we sing
   Long may our land be bright
   With freedom's holy light
   Protect us by thy might,
   Great God, our King

THE OLD GRAY MARE

Words and Music by
J. WARNER

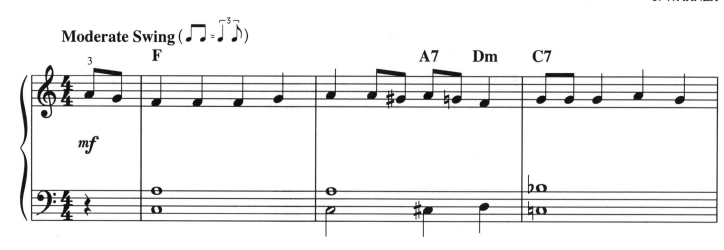

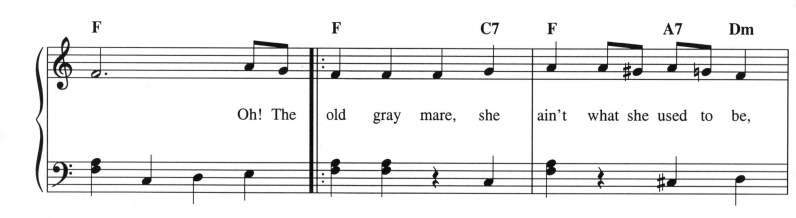

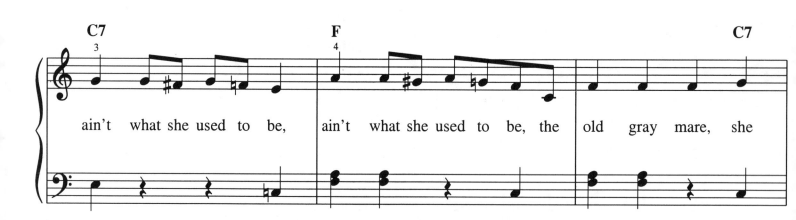

OLD MACDONALD HAD A FARM

Traditional Children's Song

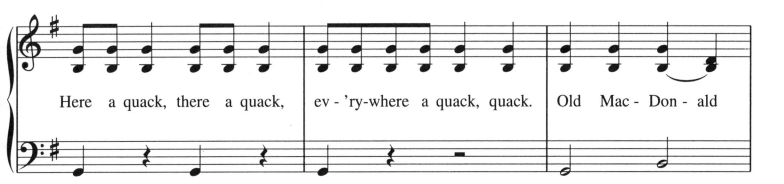

Here a quack, there a quack, ev - 'ry-where a quack, quack. Old Mac - Don - ald

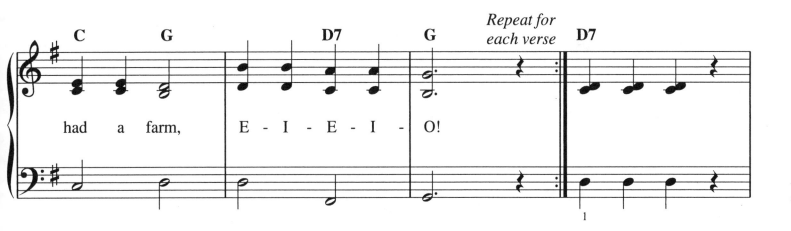

C   G   D7   G   *Repeat for each verse*   D7

had   a farm,   E - I - E - I - O!

G

Additional Lyrics

2. Old MacDonald Had a Farm,
E - I - E - I - O!
And on this farm he had a chick,
E - I - E - I - O!
With a chick, chick here
And a chick, chick there,
Here a chick, there a chick,
Everywhere a chick, chick
Old MacDonald Had a Farm,
E - I - E - I - O!

3. Other verses:

3. Cow - moo, moo
4. Dogs - bow, bow
5. Pigs - oink, oink
6. Rooster - cock-a-doodle, cock-a-doodle
7. Turkey - gobble, gobble
8. Cat - meow, meow
9. Horse - neigh, neigh
10. Donkey - hee-haw, hee-haw

PEANUT SAT ON A RAILROAD TRACK

Traditional

(like a locomotive)

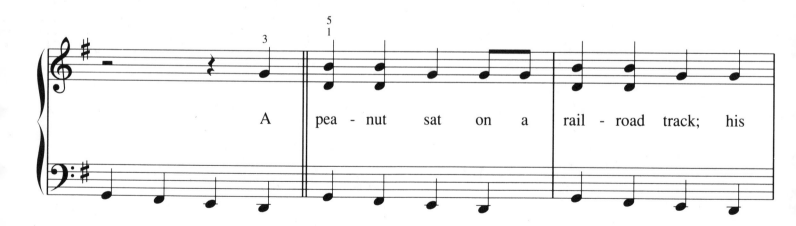

A pea - nut sat on a rail - road track; his

PEASE PORRIDGE HOT

Traditional

Moderately

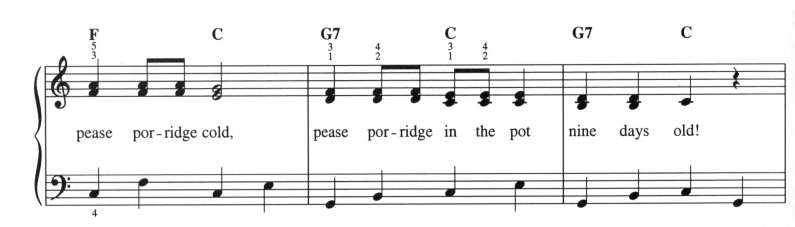

Pease por-ridge hot,

pease por-ridge cold,   pease por-ridge in the pot   nine days old!

Some like it hot,   some like it cold,   pease por-ridge in the pot   nine days   old!

SWEET BETSY FROM PIKE

American Folksong

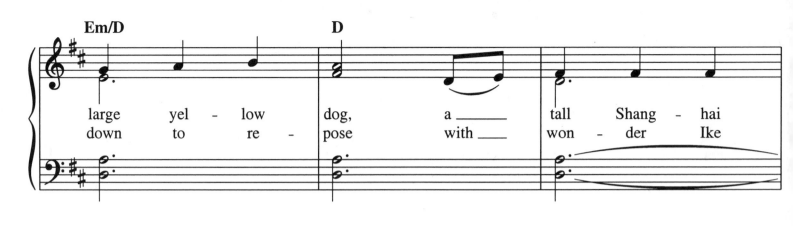

large yel - low dog, a _____ tall Shang - hai
down to re - pose with ___ won - der Ike

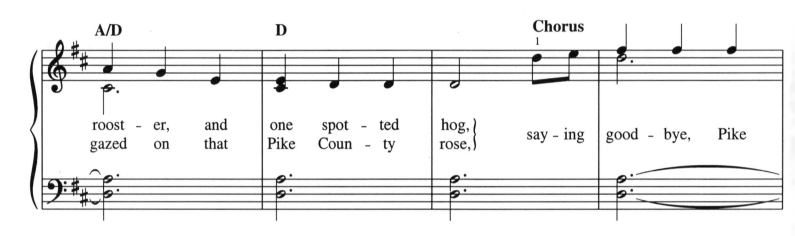

roost - er, and one spot - ted hog,} say - ing good - bye, Pike
gazed on that one Pike Coun - ty rose,}

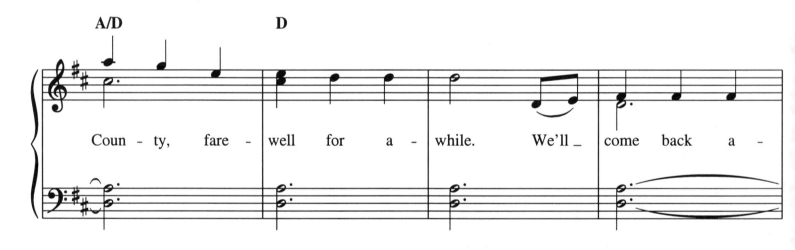

Coun - ty, fare - well for a - while. We'll _ come back a -

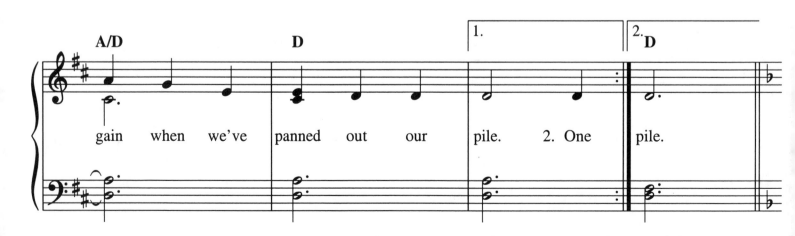

gain when we've panned out our pile. 2. One pile.

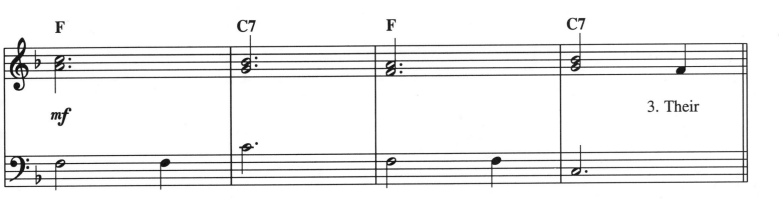

mf

3. Their

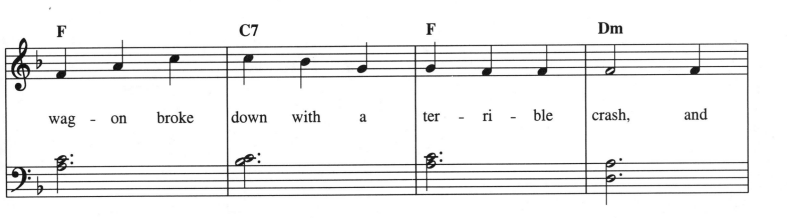

wag - on broke down with a ter - ri - ble crash, and

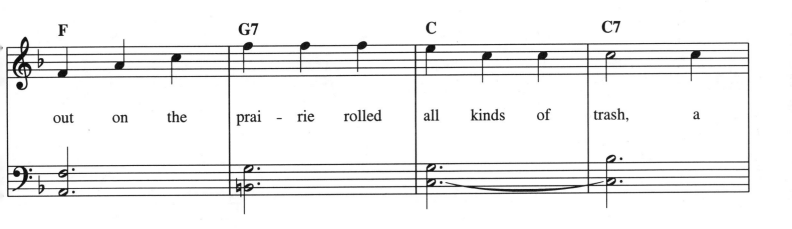

out on the prai - rie rolled all kinds of trash, a

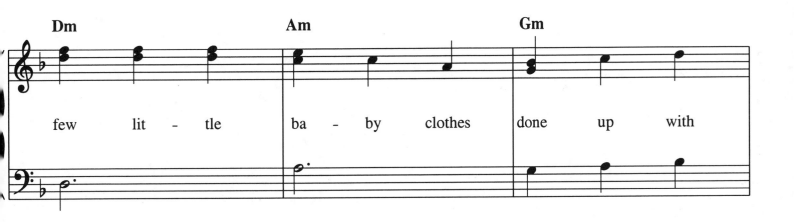

few lit - tle ba - by clothes done up with

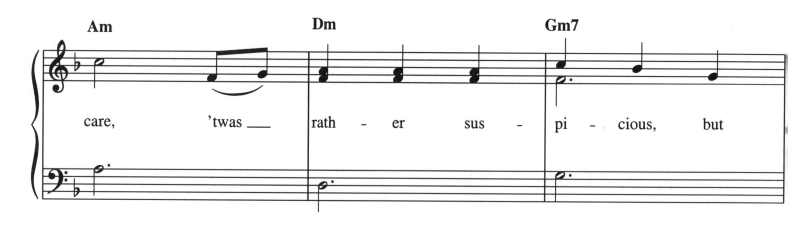

care,   'twas ___ rath - er sus - pi - cious, but

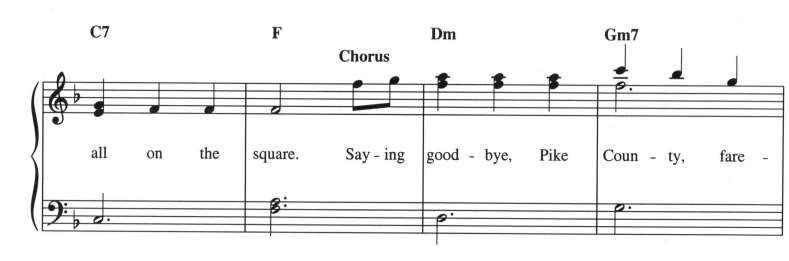

all   on   the   square.   Say - ing   good - bye,   Pike   Coun - ty,   fare -

well   for   a -   while.   We'll ___   come   back   a -

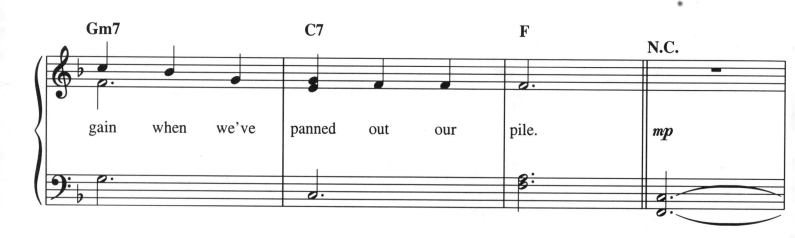

gain   when   we've   panned   out   our   pile.   *mp*

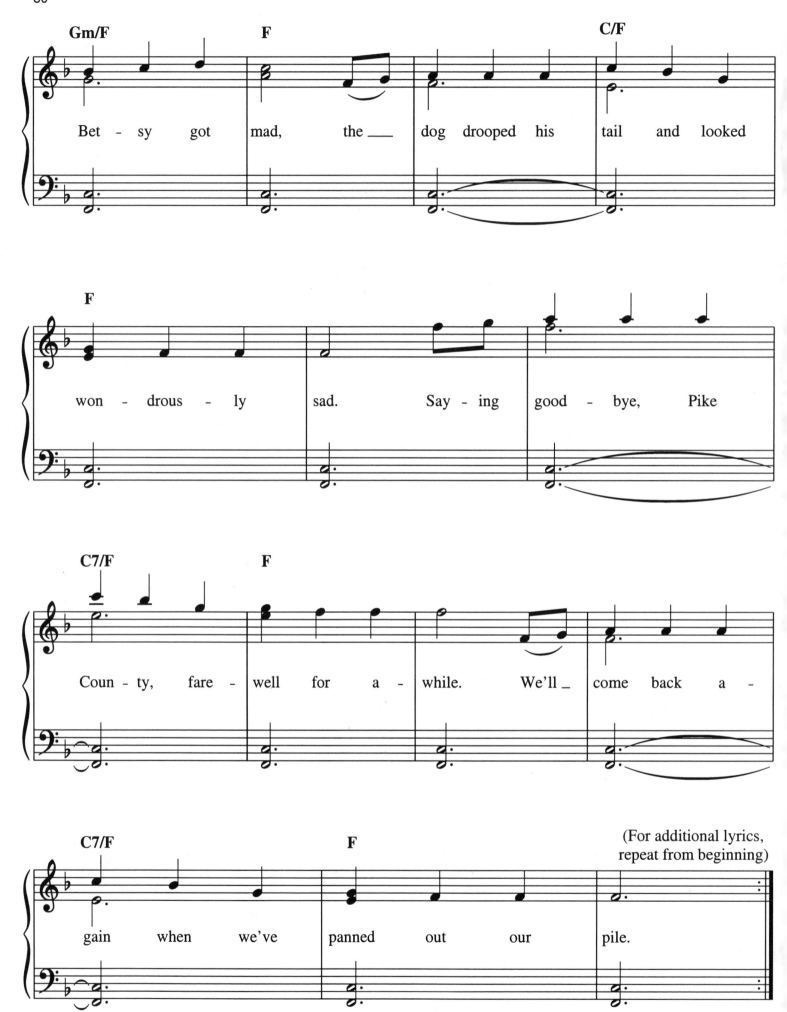

Bet - sy got mad, the ___ dog drooped his tail and looked won - drous - ly sad. Say - ing good - bye, Pike Coun - ty, fare - well for a - while. We'll _ come back a - gain when we've panned out our pile.

(For additional lyrics, repeat from beginning)

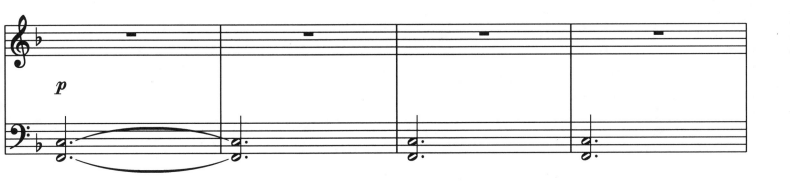

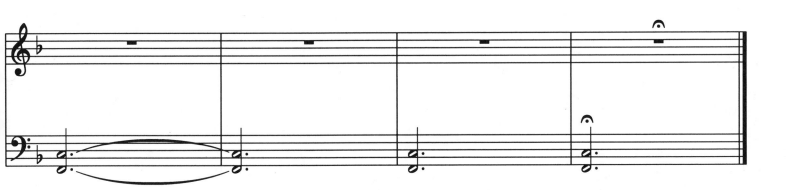

Additional Lyrics

5. They soon reached the desert where Betsy gave out,
   And down in the sand she lay rolling about;
   While Ike, half distracted, looked on with surprise,
   Saying, "Betsy, get up, you'll get sand in your eyes."
   To Chorus

6. Sweet Betsy got up in a great deal of pain,
   Declared she'd go back to Pike County again;
   But Ike gave a sigh, and they fondly embraced,
   And they traveled along with his arm 'round her waist.
   To Chorus

7. They suddenly stopped on a very high hill,
   With wonder they looked down upon old Placerville;
   Ike sighed when he said, and he cast his eyes down,
   "Sweet Betsy, my darling, we've got to Hangtown."
   To Chorus

8. Long Ike and sweet Betsy attended a dance;
   Ike wore a pair of his Pike County pants;
   Sweet Betsy was dressed up in ribbons and rings;
   Says Ike, "You're an angel, but where are your wings?"
   To Chorus

POLLY PUT THE KETTLE ON

Traditional

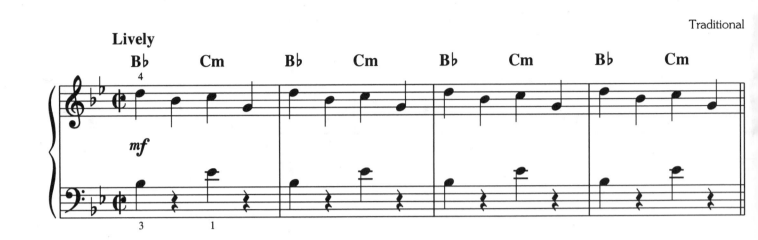

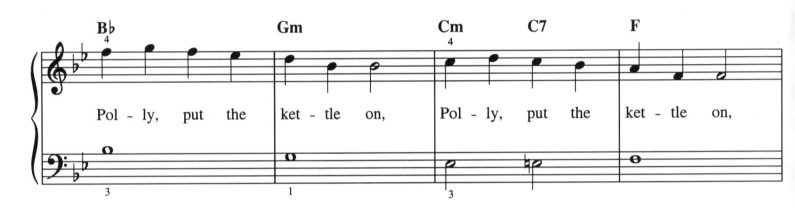

Pol - ly, put the ket - tle on, Pol - ly, put the ket - tle on,

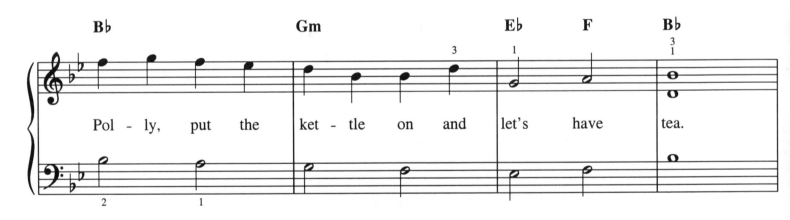

Pol - ly, put the ket - tle on and let's have tea.

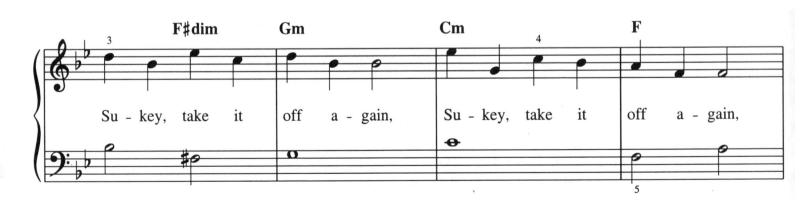

Su - key, take it off a - gain, Su - key, take it off a - gain,

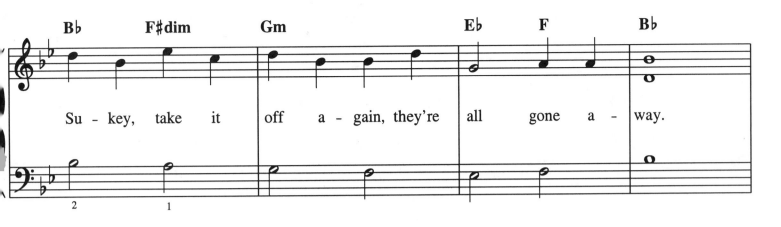

Su - key, take it off a - gain, they're all gone a - way.

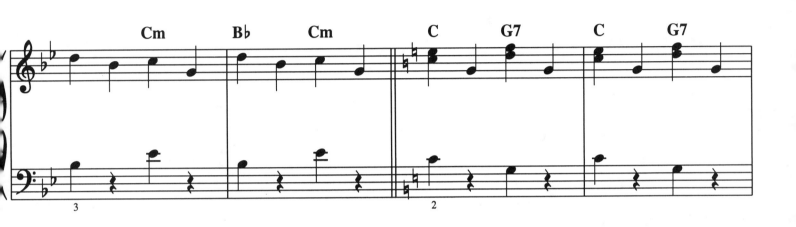

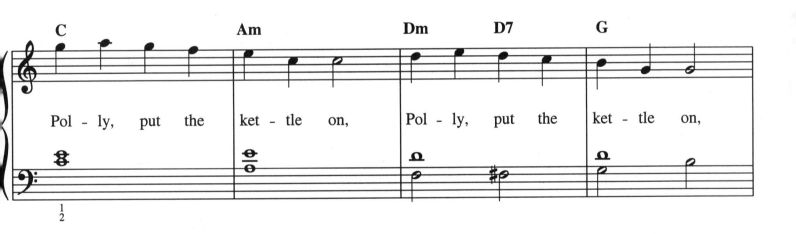

Pol - ly, put the ket - tle on, Pol - ly, put the ket - tle on,

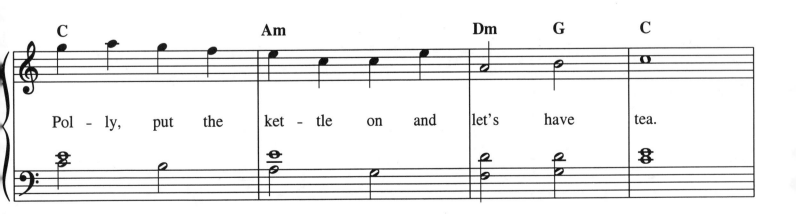

Pol - ly, put the ket - tle on and let's have tea.

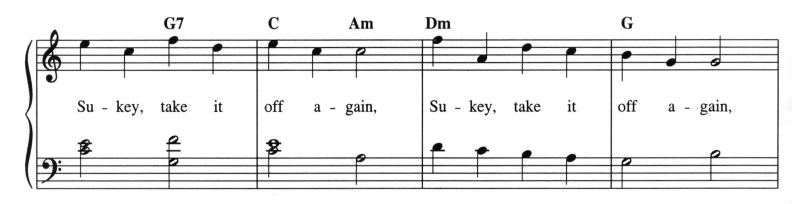

Su - key, take it off a - gain, Su - key, take it off a - gain,

Su - key, take it off a - gain, they're all gone a - way.

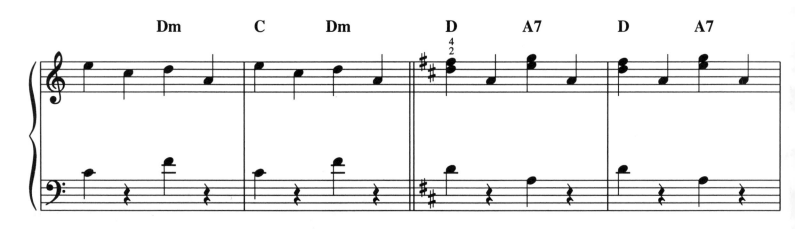

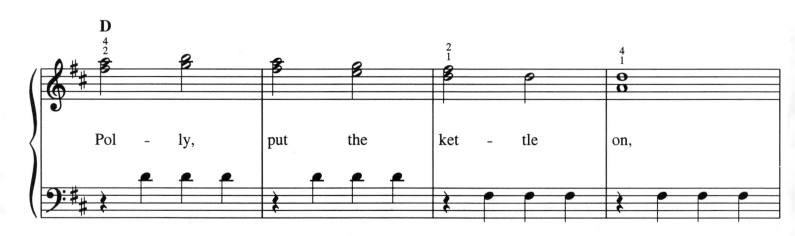

Pol - ly, put the ket - tle on,

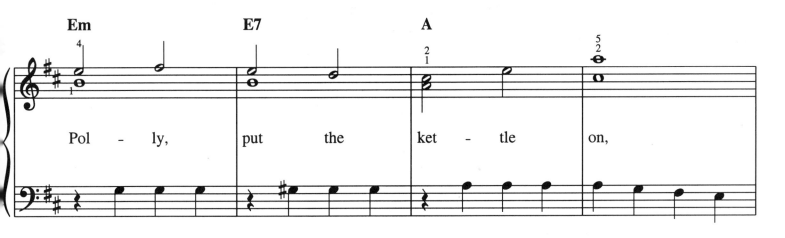

Pol - ly, put the ket - tle on,

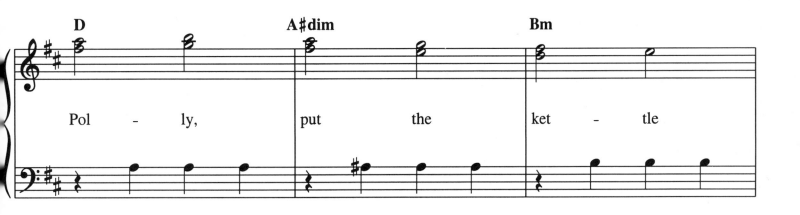

Pol - ly, put the ket - tle

on and let's have

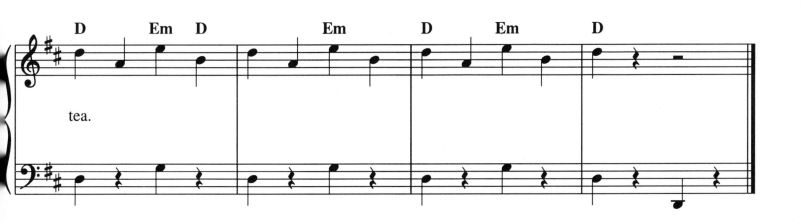

tea.

POP GOES THE WEASEL

Traditional

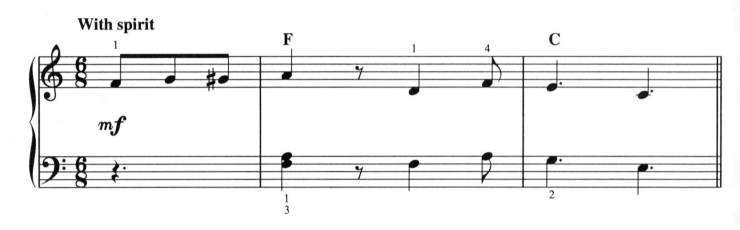

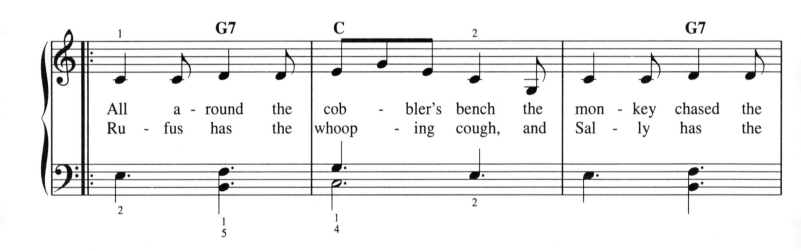

All a - round the cob - bler's bench the mon - key chased the
Ru - fus has the whoop - ing cough, and Sal - ly has the

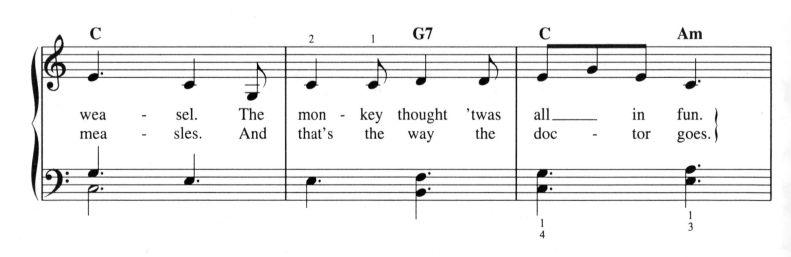

wea - sel. The mon - key thought 'twas all_____ in fun. }
mea - sles. And that's the way the doc - tor goes. }

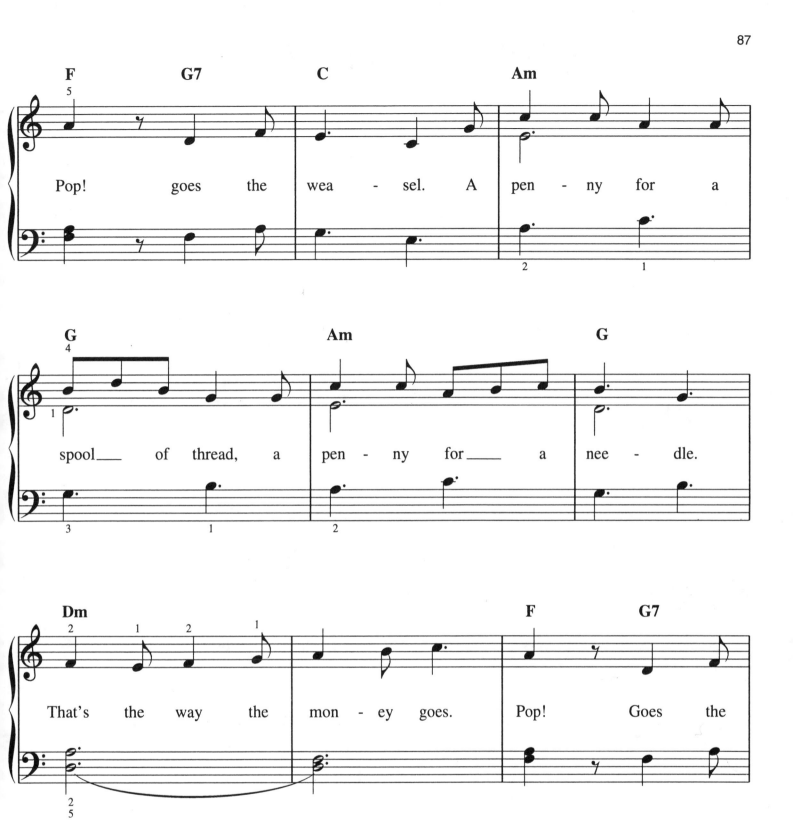

ROCK-A-BYE, BABY

Traditional

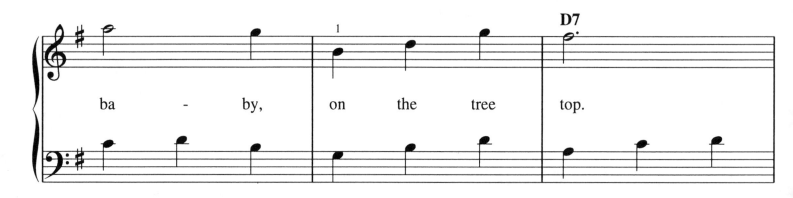

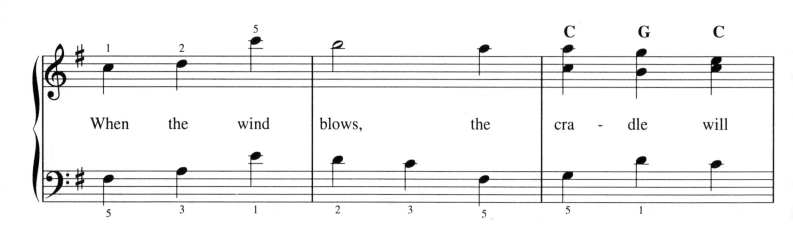

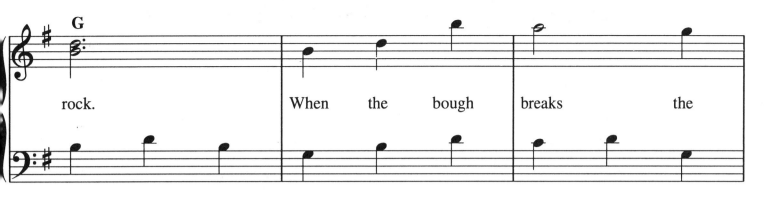

rock.   When   the   bough   breaks   the

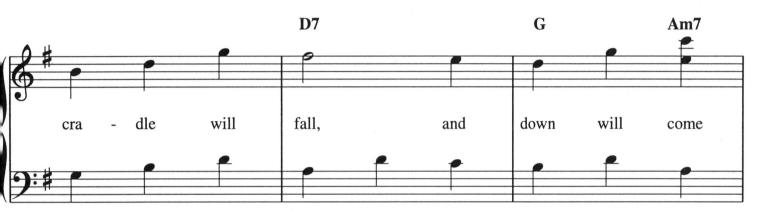

cra - dle   will   fall,   and   down   will   come

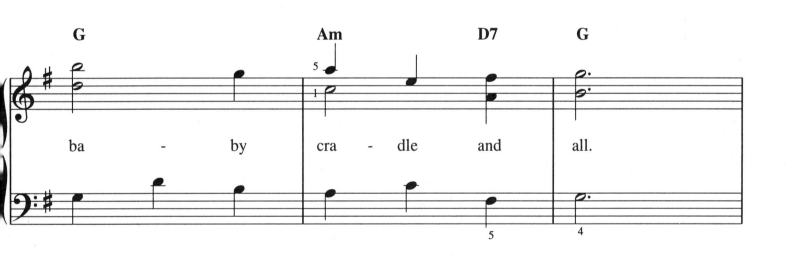

ba - by   cra - dle   and   all.

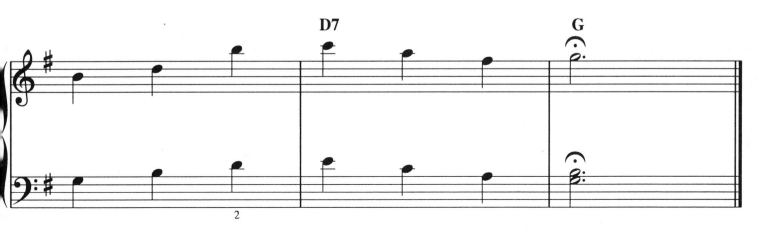

ROW, ROW, ROW YOUR BOAT

Traditional

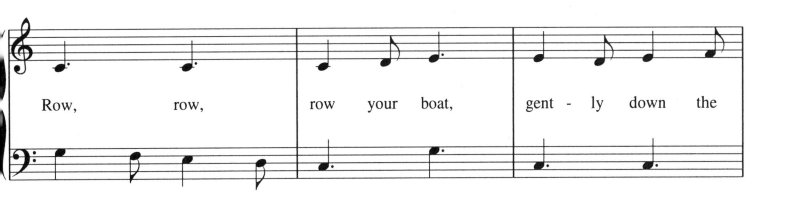

Row,   row,   row your boat,   gent - ly down the

stream.   Mer - ri - ly, mer - ri - ly,

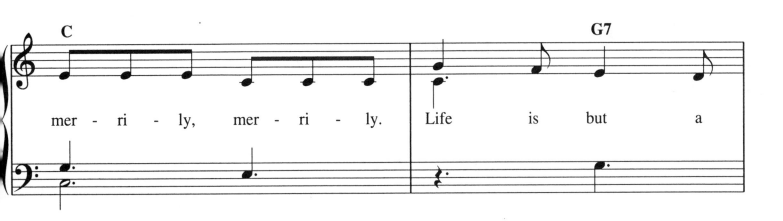

mer - ri - ly, mer - ri - ly.   Life   is   but   a

dream.

SHE'LL BE COMIN' 'ROUND THE MOUNTAIN

Traditional

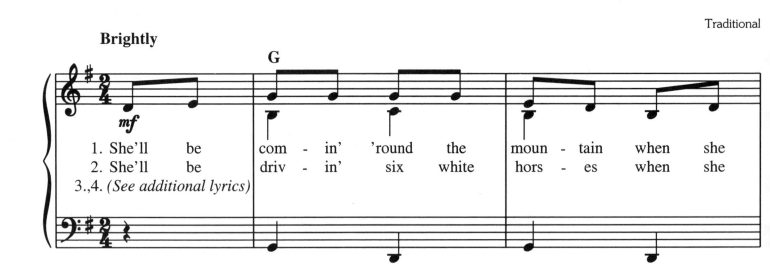

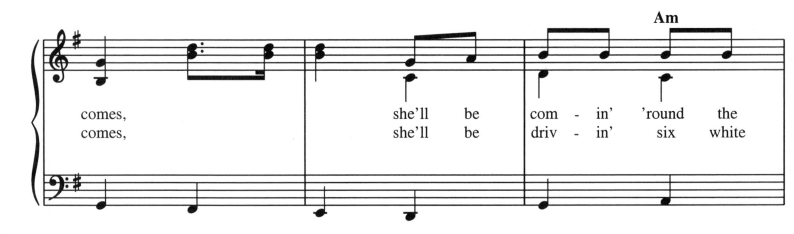

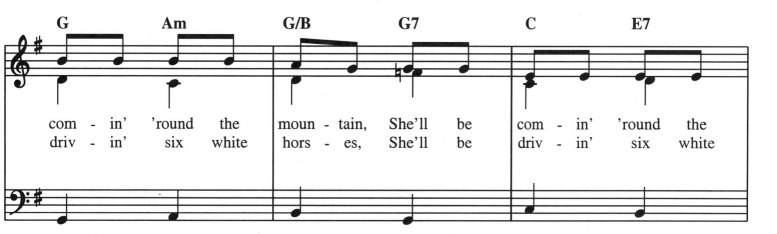

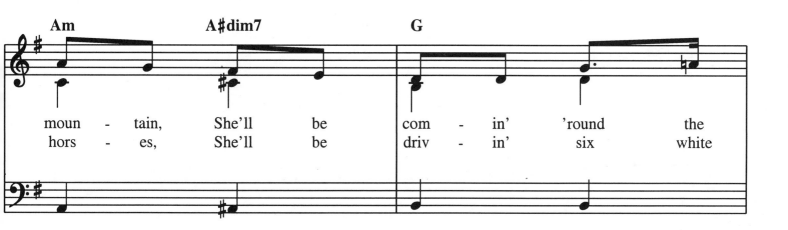

Additional Lyrics

3. Oh, we'll all go to meet her when she comes,
   Oh, we'll all go to meet her when she comes,
   Oh, we'll all go to meet her,
   Oh, we'll all go to meet her,
   Oh, we'll all go to meet her when she comes.

4. We'll be singin' "Hallelujah" when she comes,
   We'll be singin' "Hallelujah" when she comes,
   We'll be singin' "Hallelujah,"
   We'll be singin' "Hallelujah,"
   We'll be singin' "Hallelujah" when she comes.

SKIP TO MY LOU

Traditional

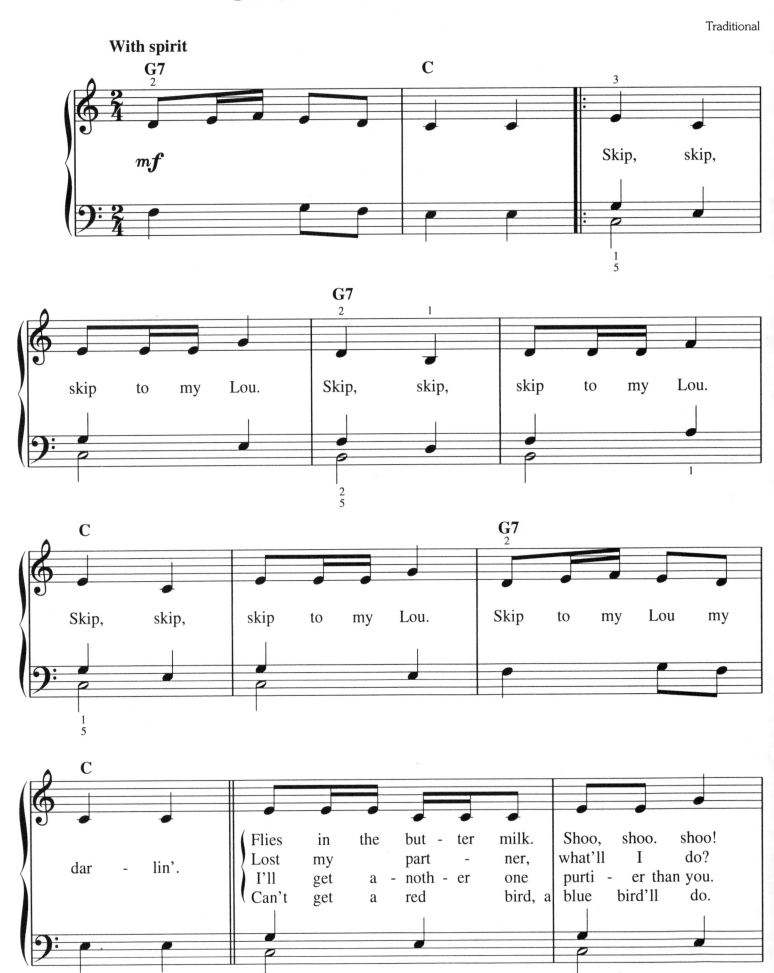

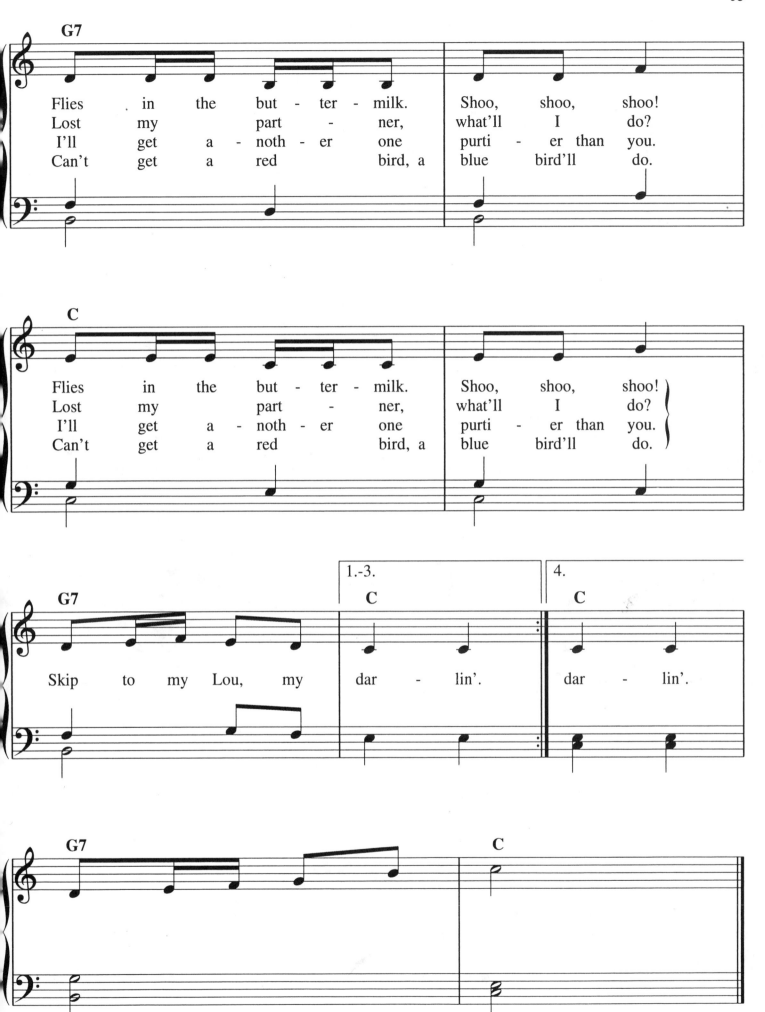

THERE'S A HOLE IN THE BUCKET

Traditional

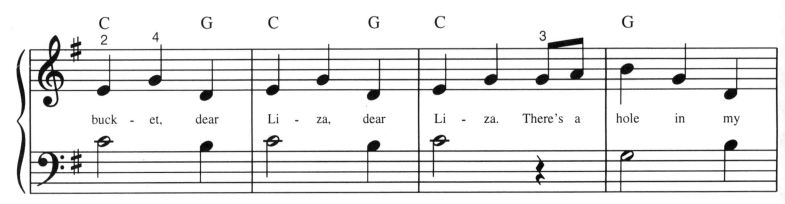

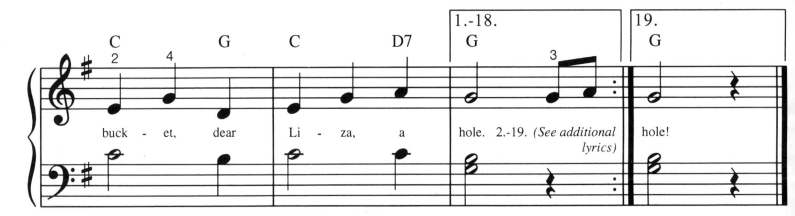

Additional Lyrics

2. Well, fix it, dear Henry, etc.
3. With what shall I fix it, dear Liza, etc.
4. With a straw, dear Henry, etc.
5. But the straw is too long, dear Liza, etc.
6. Then cut it, dear Henry, etc.
7. With what shall I cut it, dear Liza, etc.
8. With a knife, dear Henry, etc.
9. But the knife is too dull, dear Liza, etc.
10. Then sharpen it, dear Henry, etc.
11. With what shall I sharpen it, dear Liza, etc.
12. With a stone, dear Henry, etc.
13. But the stone is too dry, dear Liza, etc.
14. Then wet it, dear Henry, etc.
15. With what shall I wet it, dear Liza, etc.
16. With water, dear Henry, etc.
17. In what shall I carry it, dear Liza, etc.
18. In a bucket, dear Henry, etc.
19. There's a hole in my bucket, dear Liza, etc.

TOM, TOM, THE PIPER'S SON

Traditional

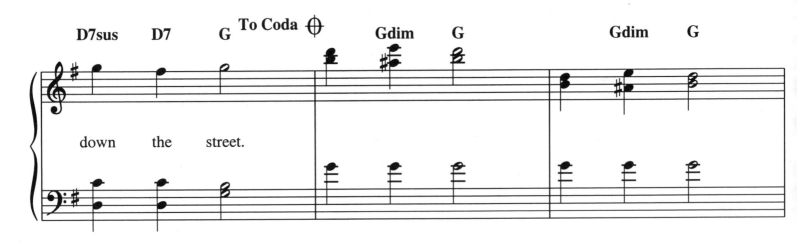

THIS LITTLE LIGHT OF MINE

African-American Spiritual

I've got the light of grace, I'm gon-na let it shine.

I've got the light of grace, I'm gon-na let it shine.

I've got the light of grace, I'm gon-na let it shine ev - 'ry

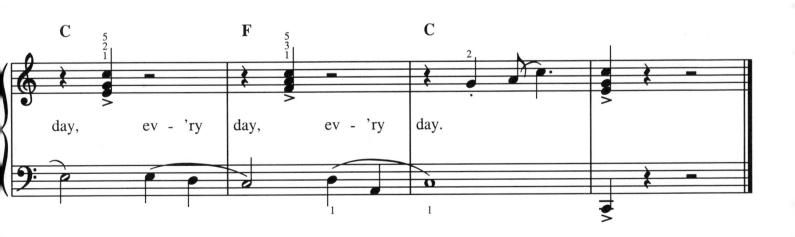

day, ev - 'ry day, ev - 'ry day.

THIS OLD MAN

Traditional

He played knick - knack on my shoe with a knick-knack, pad - dy -whack,

give the dog a bone. This old man came roll - ing home.

1.-9. C G7 C

10. G7

This old man came

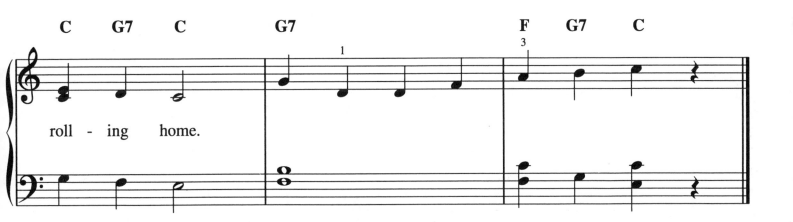

roll - ing home. This old man came

Additional Lyrics

3. This old man, he played three,
   He played knick-knack on my knee. *(Chorus)*

4. This old man, he played four,
   He played knick-knack on my door. *(Chorus)*

5. This old man, he played five,
   He played knick-knack on my hive. *(Chorus)*

6. This old man, he played six,
   He played knick-knack on my sticks. *(Chorus)*

7. This old man, he played seven,
   He played knick-knack up to heaven. *(Chorus)*

8. This old man, he played eight,
   He played knick-knack at the gate. *(Chorus)*

9. This old man, he played nine,
   He played knick-knack on my line. *(Chorus)*

10. This old man, he played ten,
    He played knick-knack over again. *(Chorus)*

THREE BLIND MICE

Traditional

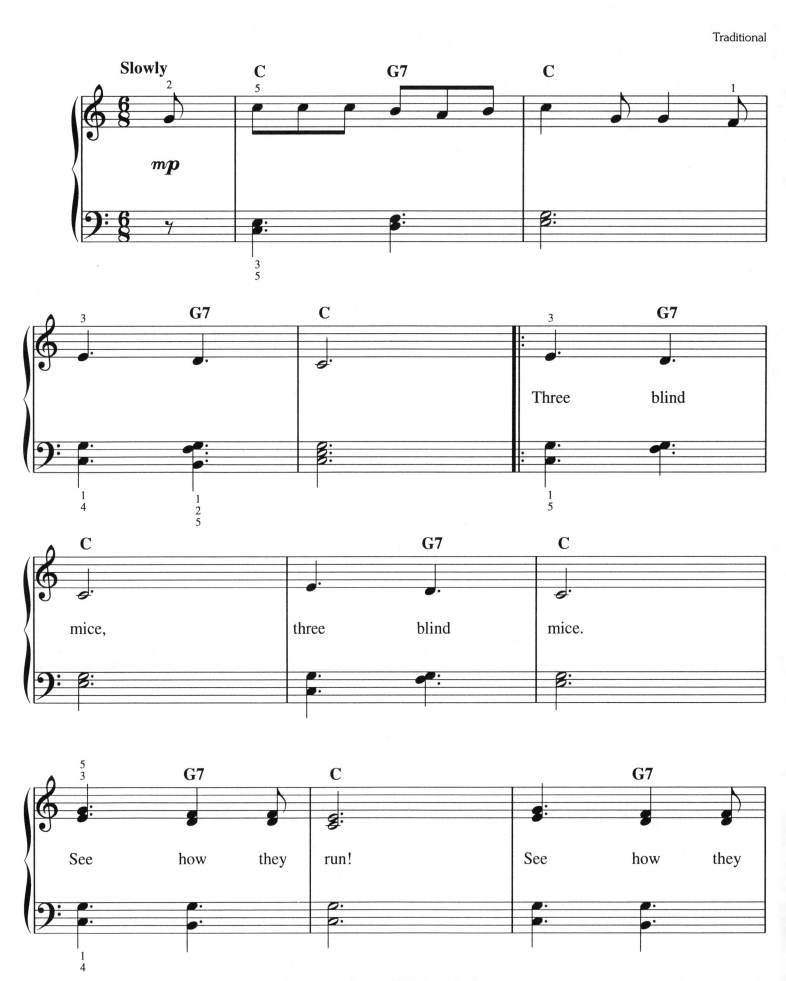

Three blind mice, three blind mice. See how they run! See how they

run!_____ They all ran af - ter the farm - er's wife, who

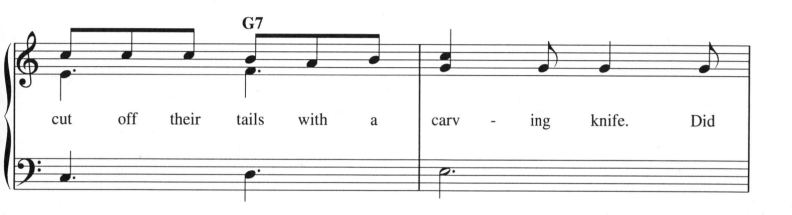

cut off their tails with a carv - ing knife. Did

you ev - er see such a sight in your life as three blind

mice.

TWINKLE, TWINKLE LITTLE STAR

Traditional

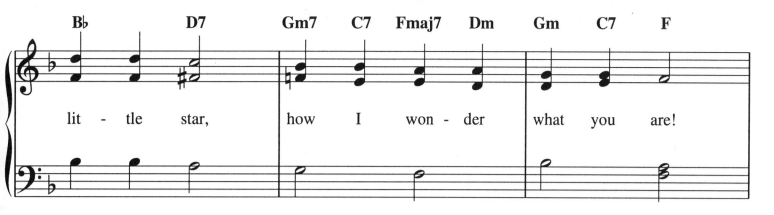

lit - tle star,   how   I   won - der   what   you   are!

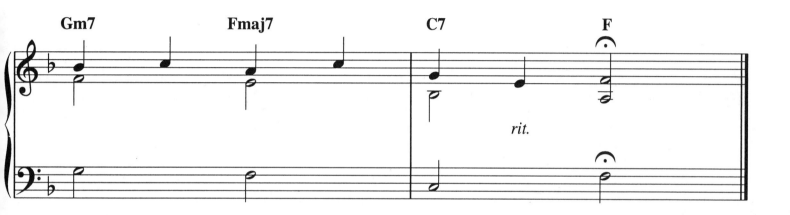

rit.

Additional Lyrics

THE ALPHABET SONG

A B C D E F G,
H I J K L M N O P,
Q R S, T U V,
W, X, Y, and Z.
Now you know my ABCs;
next time won't you sing with me?

BAA, BAA, BLACK SHEEP

Baa, baa, black sheep;
have you any wool?
"Yes, sir; yes sir.
Three bags full.
One for my master,
one for my dame,
one for the little boy
who lies in the lane."

Baa, baa, black sheep;
have you any wool?
"Yes, sir; yes sir.
Three bags full.

WHEN THE SAINTS GO MARCHING IN

Words by KATHERINE E. PURVIS
Music by JAMES M. BLACK

Bright Dixieland tempo

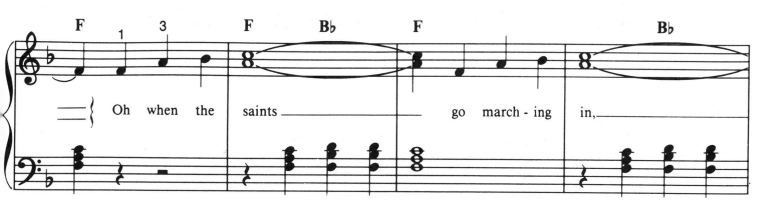

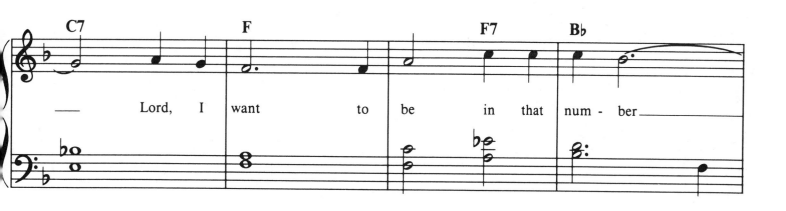

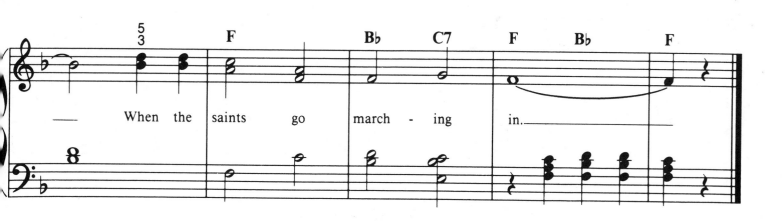

YOU'RE A GRAND OLD FLAG

Words and Music by
GEORGE M. COHAN

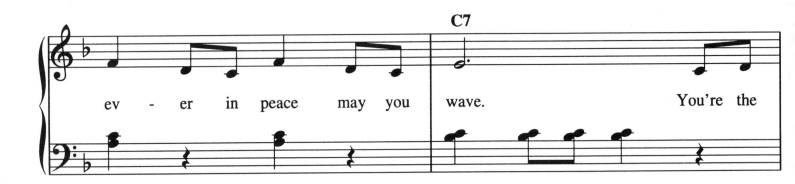

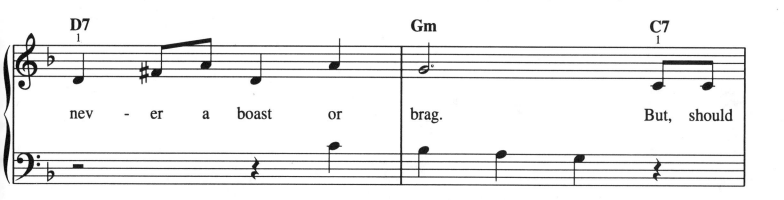

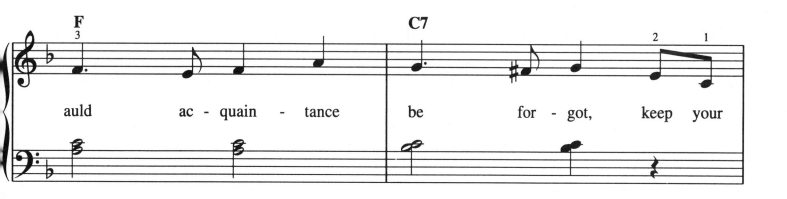

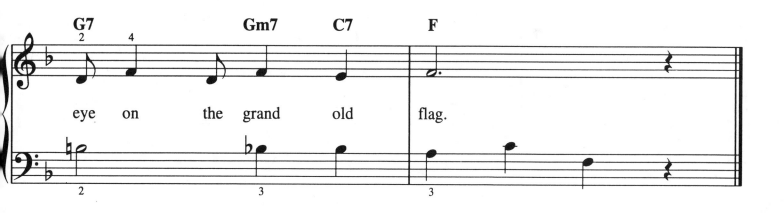

YANKEE DOODLE

Traditional